HARRISON E. SALISBURY

WITHDRAWN

the shook-up generation

Theodore Lownik Library
Illinois Benedictine College
Lisle, Illinois 60532

THE SHOOK-UP GENERATION
Copyright © 1958 by Harrison E. Salisbury
Printed in the United States of America
All rights in this book are reserved.
No part of the book may be used or reproduced in
any manner whatsoever without written permission
except in the case of brief quotations embodied in
critical articles and reviews. For information address
Harper & Row, Publishers, Incorporated,
49 East 33rd Street, New York 16, N. Y.

M-N

Library of Congress catalog card number: 58-11394

69078

For My Father and Mother

contents ——

contents

a glossary of street gang argot

A FAIR ONE *A fair fight between gangs or gang members, fought in some accordance with rules.*

BOP *To fight.*

BOPPING CLUB *A fighting gang.*

BREAD *Money (Term used mostly by drug addicts).*

BUSTED *Arrested.*

CHEESY *Traitorous.*

COOL *An uneasy armistice.*

COOLIE *Non-gang boy.*

COOL IT! *Take it easy!*

DEBS *Girl affiliates of gang boys.*

DIDDLEY BOP *First-class gang fighter.*

DIG *To understand.*

DIG IT! *Get this!*

DROP A DIME *Give me a dime.*

DUKE *To fight (with fists).*

FISH *An erotic dance similar to the burlesque house grind.*

GIG *A party.*

GO DOWN *To attack another gang, declare war.*

GRIND *An erotic dance, similar to the fish.*

HEART *Courage.*

HURT *To kill or wound seriously.*

HUSTLE *A racket (Used by drug addicts).*

JAP   *To ambush or attack an individual.*

JAZZ   *Worthless talk, poor excuse.*

JUNKIE   *Drug addict.*

MEET   *A meeting, usually of gang chiefs.*

PAD   *Room (Used by drug addicts).*

PECKS   *Food (Used by drug addicts).*

PIECE   *Gun, weapon.*

POT   *Narcotics.*

PUNK OUT   *Display cowardice.*

PUSHER   *Drug salesman.*

RANK   *To insult (Usually profanity concerning a boy's mother).*

REP   *Reputation, usually fighting reputation.*

RUMBLE   *Gang fight.*

SHAKEDOWN   *A police inspection to see if a boy is carrying weapons.*

SHIN BATTLE   *Intra-gang practice fight, sham battle.*

SHUFFLE   *To engage in a fist fight.*

SNAG   *To attack an individual, usually by surprise.*

SNAKE   *Spy*

SNEAKY PETE   *Cheap wine.*

SOUND   (Noun) *Talk, argot.* (Verb) *To joke or taunt.*

STENJER   *Alpine-style hat with narrow brim.*

SWING WITH A GANG   *To be a gang member.*

TIGHT   *Friendly, as between gangs.*

WEAK   *Bad, poor, disappointing, unconvincing.*

the
shook-up
generation

1

a walk through brooklyn

THE subway ride from Times Square to Brooklyn costs fifteen cents. It is a quick trip, just eighteen minutes from Forty-second Street to the Smith-Ninth station in Brooklyn. No visa and no passport are required.

I have made many journeys in my life as a correspondent but none more poignant than this brief excursion to Brooklyn. The first time I went it was a raw February evening and I was setting out to explore for the *New York Times* the sources of teen-age delinquency. To discover, if I could, what constituted the shook-up generation and what had shaken it so badly.

One Saturday morning in late spring I took the trip again, retracing a familiar route. By now I knew a good deal about teen-age gangs but I wanted another look at the neighborhoods I had visited. I wanted to talk, if possible, with some of the youngsters whom I had met during the winter months. I knew that I would find many of them no longer on the streets. Some were in jail, some in the hospital and some had moved away. At least one boy was dead.

In our homes, sitting before the TV of an evening, it is hard to realize the terrible swiftness with which life carries

1

the shook-up youngsters toward tragedy, disaster and death.

On this Saturday morning the Coney Island Express was not crowded. Across from me sat a faded blonde in dark glasses and tan spring coat. She was reading a Greek Orthodox church paper. I made out the headline: "War with Russia Inevitable." She glanced at it and turned the page. In a seat ahead was a slim, dark-haired girl, not more than twenty-one, wearing glove-tight gray slacks, white bobby socks, black dance pumps and an Italian black-and-white knit sweater. The headline on her paper said something about a teen-age gang shooting.

Teen-age gang shooting . . . There were not many days of the week, I thought, when a newspaper did not have a choice of teen-age violence to exploit. The teen-age problem and the Russian problem—there was, I suspected, a somewhat closer connection between the great issues of our times than many imagined. They might, even, be regarded as two faces of one coin—the conflicts that grew in the tainted soil of neglect at home and the conflicts abroad with their deep roots in social and political neglect on a wider scale.

Perhaps, I thought, if our democracy could be made to work better at home we would not encounter so many crises abroad.

For lack of better occupation I let my eyes rove over the subway advertising cards. "Help Build a Boy's Future by Being a Big Brother," I read. "Inspiration, Guidance, Friendship." Fine sentiments. But how many persons would be stirred to action. An adjoining ad pictured a girl with low-cut peasant blouse. "New Economy Fares to Europe," the card said. It would not be difficult, I thought, for a Madison Avenue motivational research team to demonstrate that pretty girls arouse more interest in pleasure trips to Europe than do plain, honest words concerning the future of our boys. And yet the day was nearing when the security and fate of our country would depend on maximum mobilization of all our human talents and resources.

There is not, it seemed to me, a very close correlation between what we need to do and what we actually do.

Another card drew my attention. "Cheyenne Never Misses," an ad for the classified telephone directory. Cheyenne was a favorite gang name. I knew a boy named Cheyenne who was trying to break away from street life. He was eighteen years old and he had a steady girl. A nice, serious girl who worked in Manhattan as a stenographer. They were talking about getting married but the chances were that Cheyenne was not going to make it. At this moment he was sitting in Raymond Street jail, awaiting a hearing on a Sullivan Act charge. He had been picked up with a gun in his pocket. Since he was already on parole the least he could expect was a year in prison. Whether his quiet, serious Dottie would still be waiting for him after he had spent a year in Elmira was doubtful. Whether he would still be interested in going straight after a year in Elmira was even more doubtful. It was a bad break for Cheyenne that he had happened to be picked up with a "piece" on him. But, as his friends said, "that's the way the little ball bounces."

Within a few minutes the Coney Island Express pulled out of Borough Hall station, Brooklyn. Three minutes more and we roared out of the underground and up a steep incline into the gray sunlight of a hazy day. The train climbed the steel trestle high over the forest of red and brown buildings that tumbled across the landscape. Close at hand loomed two great black gas tanks. A block away the tubular monstrosity of Gowanus Super-Highway bestrode the city like a giant's trampoline.

This was south Brooklyn, a crowded territory, jammed between the white limestone towers of Borough Hall, the jagged steel fretwork of Navy Yard and the sawtooth of Red

Hook, Erie Basin and Greenpoint. Here and there among
the row houses and tenements rose eight- or ten-story plants
and warehouses of reinforced concrete, once painted white
but long since chipped and fading.

The train swept into the great curve of Smith-Ninth
Street station and ground to a grudging halt. This is the
highest elevated station in New York City. From the platform I looked back—dim in the foggy distance was the gleam
of Wall Street's spires and the lacy East River bridges. I
looked down into the tenement back yards, the rubbish
piles and paper tatters brightened by wash lines of blue
and pink, purple and yellow. Here and there I saw the
scraggly green of the Brooklyn back-yard trees, dwarfed by
soot and sickened by cinders.

Not many persons got off the train at Smith-Ninth and
they headed down the long staircase and two flights of narrow
oaken escalators without a glance. I followed more slowly.
I had not been in the neighborhood for weeks and I wanted
to catch up on the news.

The platform and stair walls of the Smith-Ninth station
are covered with what first appears to be an embroidery of
white chalk, red paint and black crayon. The tracery of lines
is everywhere but it is not embroidery. It is a living newspaper of the streets. Here are the threats and taunts of rival
gangs, the challenges and defiances. Here is word of neighborhood romance, old flames and new loves. Here bids are
staked for leadership. Here bulletins are posted on the
rumbles.

On one wall I read these scrawlings: Joan & Atlas, Joan
and the Boy who works in Spilmans, Gogi, Sal and Annie,
China, Quo Vadis, Ditmas Dukes, Bull and the El Vilows,
Bull & Peaches, Bull & Pat, Bull. Bull was new to me. It
appeared that he was making an impact in the neighborhood.

Another panel offered more sinister intelligence.

It read:

JOE L. FINALLY GOT HIS

ASTORIA TRAMPS

HOBO LORDS

I didn't know to which Joe the message referred but it sounded as though street justice had been meted out.

Nearby was a challenge:

CHICAGOS CAPONE

DEE-FIES ANY

NEW YORK HOOD

MAKE A DATE

Social notes covered one wall: Flame of Amazon Jrs., Latin Aces of Fort Green—Porky, Jane, Carols, Snookie, Bobo, Butch, Johnny Q. I guessed that some youngsters from the Fort Greene Housing Project had paid a call on their Red Hook neighbors.

Beside the stairway were a variety of notations: China of the El Kovan Ladies, Shorty of the El Kovan Ladies, Home of El Kovans, Obey His Holy Law, Red Hook Boys, Support Mental Health, Vici of the Dark Doves was Here, Dee Dee of the Imperial Queens was Here (Brother club of Imperial Nites), Rico, Nero, Jolly Boy, Sharkey—El Kovans, Syntheea was Here.

Some of these names were familiar to me. Some were not. Once again I was struck by what seems a curious fact. On these walls there was no pornography, no outhouse drawings, no scatology.

Above the staircase I saw written a sentence in very fresh white chalk. It read:

ALL GOWANUS WILL GET FUCKED UP IF LEROY DIES.

That sentence had been chalked only last night or this

morning. I knew this because I knew who Leroy was and I knew why the message had been scrawled. In fact, there was a story about Leroy in the paper which I held in my hand. He was the latest casualty of teen-age warfare in the city streets, newest victim of the violence of the shook-up generation. It was because of Leroy and the thousands of youngsters like him that I had made the acquaintance of Red Hook, Fort Greene, Bedford-Stuyvesant, East Harlem, the lower East Side, the upper West Side and other breakdown areas where extreme patterns of adolescent antisocial behavior can be observed.

There was little unusual in Leroy's case, except, possibly, the fact that he was still alive. Two nights ago the police had been put on the alert. A rumble, or gang fight, it was rumored, was set for about 9 P.M. Squad cars constantly prowl the dingy blocks of south Brooklyn. More were ordered into the area.

Leroy is a Negro boy, fourteen years old, large for his age. He lives with his widowed mother in Red Hook Houses, a great public housing project just two blocks from Smith-Ninth Street station. That evening he was standing outside a neighborhood center in Gowanus when an officer noticed a bulge under his tight-fitting jacket. The bulge was a zip gun, loaded with a .22-caliber cartridge.

The officer took the gun from Leroy. A second policeman came up and made Leroy put his hands behind him. He slipped a pair of handcuffs over the boy's wrists. What happened next depends on whose story you believe. The officers say Leroy slipped from their grasp and dashed up the street. One officer drew his pistol and gave chase. He fired three shots. One, he said, was a "warning." Then he stumbled and his gun went off twice more "by accident." All three bullets found their way into Leroy's body. He fell, dangerously wounded.

"Why did they shoot?" his mother asked. "How far did they think he would get with his hands in handcuffs behind his back?" At the hospital Leroy's mother insisted that he was a good boy, that he did well in school, that she had hoped for him to go to college, that he must have found the zip gun in the street, that he never belonged to a gang. I could imagine what she felt. A thousand parents have wept at the bedsides of their boys. Always, they say, he was a good boy. He was not a bad boy. He had never been in trouble. He didn't belong to a gang. And most of the parents believed what they said—with their hearts even when their minds told them differently. They were one with the parents in Scarsdale, New York, when the bad news came from the police about Dicky. Dicky never drank. Dicky never ran around with a bad crowd. He was doing well in school. How could he have been the boy who drove the hit-and-run car that killed the little girl? Not Dicky. Not our Dicky.

So it had been with Leroy and his mother. I studied the chalk notice above the staircase. It cast some light on the incident. The rumble against which the police had been alerted was supposed to involve Red Hook boys and Gowanus boys. The chalk notice implied that the Red Hook gang regarded Leroy as one of theirs. It warned the Gowanus gang that it would be held responsible in case of Leroy's death. Here was the whole murderous mechanism of street gangism, naked and exposed. One boy killed—another must die. An eye for an eye. A life for a life.

I thought of Leroy as I rode down the long escalator and walked out into the street, past two women selling *The Watchtower,* one in English, one in Spanish. There was little to distinguish Leroy from a hundred youngsters I had met in street conflict areas. So far as I knew he was a typical product of his age and his environment. His father was dead. This did not set him apart. Few of his friends had fathers in the home. I knew the boys he hung out with at the Community Center and I knew those he went to school with at Boys' High School. Other youngsters with the same background. They would say that it was tough luck for

Leroy to be shot down by a cop but what did you expect from the sons-of-bitches? They would not be surprised that something bad had happened to Leroy. That was what happened to these boys every day. If you managed to get through today it was better not to think about tomorrow. Leroy lived in Red Hook Houses. He could just as well have lived in a Harlem tenement. Or he could have grown up in Chicago's South Side or in the slattern slums of Gary, Indiana, or South San Francisco. The outcome would have been just about the same.

I walked down Ninth Street. Many a time Leroy must have walked these two short blocks between towering subway station and the bluish-steel obscenity of Gowanus Super-Highway. So many times that his eyes no longer would notice the rubbish cans beside each neat, red-brick, three-story house or the empty whiskey bottles in the doorways.

Perhaps his eye might have been caught by two bushel baskets of plaster-of-Paris figures outside the grocery. One was filled with offal-pink, life-sized little pigs with golden ears. The other with mud-brown, life-sized baby gorillas with mouths that were lipstick-red. Take your choice. Take one of each. Only $1.29.

A boy who lives in Red Hook Houses keeps on the alert as he walks from the subway to the project. He is ready to run for his life at any moment. The reason is simple. The route from subway to project is controlled by a gang that lives outside Red Hook Houses. This gang is at war with the boys inside the project. These two blocks of innocent brick fronts have been the scene of bloody ambushes, night assaults, pitched battles with gun, broken bottle and knife.

As I crossed Court Street I said hello to a girl whom I had met during the winter. Her name was Grace. She was a buxom plain girl of fifteen with a direct way of talking. She had called me "that reporter from the *News.*" This tabloid picture paper is about the only publication which is "read" in this area and it was her natural assumption that any newspaper reporter must be from the *News.*

Last winter this girl's fourteen-year-old brother was arrested for snatching a woman's purse. The family was in despair. They had been put on notice of eviction from the housing project and had no idea where to go. I wondered whether they had found a place to live. Flats are at a premium in this region of run-down bars, greasy spoons, candy stores with dirty windows. This area has been a slum for years but key money for a flat runs to $300 or more. Street gangs are no novelty here. The docks and the Navy Yard are not far away.

A generation ago the Red Hook Boys, the Navy Street Boys, the Garfield Boys, and the Coney Island Boys ruled the region with fist and brick and stick. The Garfield Boys were the toughest. They used to haul ashcans of cinders and broken glass up to the roofs of the four-story houses and dump them on passers-by.

New York City's Police Commissioner Stephen P. Kennedy grew up in nearby Greenpoint. The Greenpoint gangs were no sissies, either.

"In those days," the Commissioner once told me, "there was a group called the Kent Street Savages. I remember they killed a police lieutenant named Kelly. They pushed a chimney over on him. But that was an isolated incident. The problem is worse today."

The problem, I thought, is undoubtedly worse today. But it was worse than that in the more distant past. A hundred years ago whole areas of New York were held in the grip of street gangs like the Hudson Dusters, the Forty Thieves, the Dead Rabbits, the Plug Uglies, the Swamp Angels and the Slaughter Housers.

These gangs fought savage battles in the streets. A death toll of fifteen or twenty was not uncommon. Even the police feared to enter some neighborhoods. There is an impression today that the street gangs of the past were "adult" gangs whereas those of today are "adolescent" gangs. This is a misconception. One hundred years ago little distinction was made between adolescent and adult. A boy strong enough to work was regarded as an adult. Boys of fourteen or fifteen started out in life on their own. Physical maturity and strength, not chronological age, were the test. The street gangs of the last century were made up of the same age groups as those of today. This is not the first era in which society, particularly the adolescent segment, has been badly disturbed and shaken up.

To walk through Red Hook is to walk bloody ground, redolent of street combat. I paused not far from the big housing project. All was peaceful now but in this street there had been countless battles. Not many Saturdays ago at a Brooklyn movie house a boy was critically wounded by a shot from a zip gun. Three boys snapped pistols at him—only one went off. A boy named Cocoa was held in jail for firing the shot but I had been told that he was the wrong boy. He had tried to shoot the youngster but his zip gun misfired. Perhaps the rubber bands that activated the firing pin were not strong enough. Nevertheless, police had arrested Cocoa. The boy who actually fired the shot had not come forward even though his buddy was still in the hands of the law. Comradeship on the street stops at the door of the police station.

At one movie house when gangs attend performances they sit on opposite sides of the house. Bouncers watch for trouble and police squads are on call. Nevertheless, it is a rare Saturday which passes without some incident.

I followed a quiet street, leading away from Red Hook Houses, down toward the docks. Ahead were the wharfs, grim and empty on a Saturday. Here were a quiet church and a fine-looking parochial school. Here were drugstores and candy shops, dozing in the Saturday-morning peace. I saw few drinkers in the half-dozen bars. It was still too early. At the corner stood an empty store—once a favorite gang hangout. Now it was closed by the police. I had heard a dozen stories as to why it had been shut down. On the side streets more rows of three-story houses, most of them owned and occupied by their owners. Red petunias bloomed from window boxes. Here and there a garden had been planted in the back yard. But this small-town atmosphere, I knew, was deceptive. These blocks constituted the "turf" of a well-known street gang. No one on this street is surprised to hear shots ring out after dark. Or to see grim-faced, leather-jacketed youngsters leap into cars and roar off in the direction of Red Hook Houses. More than one boy has been brought home from a Saturday-night dance with a knife wound in his abdomen. The whine of the call ambulance is often heard on pleasant summer evenings.

You cannot walk these streets without seeing the signs of social deterioration which nourishes gang conflict. Here are the drink cadgers, lounging hopefully outside the afternoon bars, the flashy girls looking for a pickup, the sagging lintels of rotting houses, the pimps with their mincing gait and diamond rings, the street-corner teen-agers, idling the hours away.

These symptoms are not peculiar to one region. Take a bus over to Bedford-Stuyvesant. Here you can count as many as sixteen store-front Pentecostal churches in some blocks, separated here and there by a bar or liquor store. Here you can see the prowl cars slowly moving down the streets, the refuse spilling into the gutters, the gleam of flattened beer tins on the pavement, the rotten smell of decaying buildings, the vacant store windows blindly facing dingy streets. No area of New York has more need of public facilities than Bedford-Stuyvesant. No area has fewer. Instead, the city masses its police lest the Bedford-Stuyvesant situation "get out of hand." Nowhere will you find a heavier concentration of police than in Bedford-Stuyvesant. Nowhere are the police quicker to wield their nightsticks on street-corner youngsters. Nowhere are more youngsters jailed for "unlawful assembly." And nowhere is there more gang activity.

Bedford-Stuyvesant is a Negro ghetto, largely created in the last twenty years. Bedford-Stuyvesant gangs are all Negro. There are no other ethnic groups on which to draw. Here Negro gang bops with Negro gang. Here is a laboratory demonstration that geography and propinquity—not racial differences—lie at the heart of street combat.

This is not to say that street combat does not frequently pit a predominantly Negro gang against a group largely made up of whites. Or the battle line may be drawn between Puerto Ricans and Italians. Or Mexicans and whites of mixed origin. But usually the ethnic or race factor arises from the accident of segregated housing, low-income migration or population displacement. For the most part white gang boys fight Negro gang boys not because their skin is colored black but because they live "in the Project" or on the other side of some real or imaginary line.

You can walk from Bedford-Stuyvesant to Prospect Park in twenty minutes. On this spring day the green lawns and leafing trees of the park made a lovely splash against the brownstone barrens that surround it. I watched the children playing on clean asphalt playgrounds, the softball games on the sanded diamonds, the busy tennis courts. I wondered whether the park was as peaceful as it looked. I wondered whether the four leather-jacketed youngsters lounging beside the Pritchard Square entrance were just killing time or whether some meaning lay behind the shifting glances they directed at every passer-by. Perhaps they had nothing better to do. But perhaps they were a scout detail, watching for someone.

For a decade or more Prospect Park has not been the pleasant place of rest and relaxation which its appearance suggests. Not since the gangs began to take it over for their rumbles. Today the situation is not so bad as a few years ago. Then, on some summer evenings, two hundred or three hundred youngsters, armed with zip guns, revolvers, knives and other weapons fought it out on the greensward. A score of youngsters have been sent to the hospital after such a fight. How many have been killed no one knows. The figures aren't kept that way.

The world that produces the street gang is a limited world. Most of these adolescents have a horror of home. They call it "prison." I have visited some of these "homes" and I share the horror. Often, these youngsters have never known a real home. They have been reared by an aunt, a distant relative or friend of their vanished parents. Usually, the father is absent. In many cases there is a procession of "uncles" moving in and out.

These are adolescents born to transiency. They start in Florida, move to Georgia, move to North Carolina, move to New York City. They live in East Harlem, move to the West Side, move to the Bowery, move to the housing project. Three or four changes a year are not unusual.

For such youngsters school is a torture. Few can read. They gravitate into "slow learner" classes. They populate the manual training courses. Auto repair and printing are too complex. They have no idea why they break into the community center on Sunday, tip over the desks, smash the lights, tear down the bulletin board and rip up the pool tables. The center has been provided to give them a chance for recreation off the streets. They go there every evening. There is no place where they enjoy themselves more. Then, some dull and endless Sunday, a youngster proposes that they bust up the joint. In five minutes they are hoisting a small boy up to the high rear window, carelessly left unlocked. In another five the gang is inside, ravaging the rooms like savages. Indeed, at that moment they are savages.

When the community house director confronts them on Monday afternoon they twist their mouths sullenly: "You always blame us. We never did it. Go ahead if you want to—kick us out."

These are the boys who slip in the side door of the bar-and-grill and sit drinking their Cokes beside two teen-age prostitutes, never giving them a glance. When the proprietor tells them to leave because the squad cop is due for his nightly check-up they go without a word. No one could be better behaved.

"I don't know what's a-matter over to the center," the proprietor says. "These kids never give me no trouble."

These are the boys who turn a schoolroom into a gang arena. These are the boys who make zip guns in the carpenter shop while the teacher is showing the class how to make a tie rack. These are the boys who knife the monitor in the hall and attack the teacher who tries to bring them to order.

These are the boys who killed a teen-age paralytic named Farmer when they encountered him in a deserted park near the George Washington Bridge one summer evening, slashing his body with their knife blades and ripping his flesh with their brass-tipped garrison belts. And these are the boys whose explosion of violence caused the 1958 crisis in the New York City public schools and a grand jury inquiry which led to the suicide of a broken-hearted high school principal.

These are the boys who extort "protection" money from younger children, who rape a fourteen-year-old girl in a school corridor and shoot each other with Beretta pistols in the schoolyard.

These are the youngsters whose conflict with society is deep, relentless and unending. These are the youngsters who clog the youth courts, the youth detention houses, the reformatories and corrective institutions. They cost society a pretty penny—$5,000 or $6,000 a year in the institutions to which they are sent. Often the cost runs even higher.

In the country as a whole such youngsters constitute only a tiny fraction of the total adolescent population—a small fraction of 1 per cent. In New York City the highest police estimate of "dangerous youths" is only eight or nine thousand. A careful survey of gangs and youth groupings in a sample area of Harlem found that only one gang out of ten, even in a severely deprived area, had a definitely antisocial orientation. The same percentages hold true in samplings of youth groups in Los Angeles and Chicago. It is entirely natural and perfectly normal for youngsters to form gangs and clubs in their adolescent years. But when youngsters are shook-up, when their social rootings are insecure, their gang groups quickly can assume deep antisocial tendencies. In New York City the police estimate that just behind the critical group of "dangerous" youths stands another hundred thousand youngsters who live on the verge of trouble. They have been tabbed by police officers for truancy or loitering or trivial breaches of the peace. These are youngsters who may at any time be drawn into grave antisocial conduct by their peers. Our delinquency problem extends outward from these inner groups of troubled chidren and is capable, at any time, of touching the lives of tens of thousands of youngsters who live in wholesome normal environments.

Youngsters are impressionable and imitative. At no age is the desire to emulate more strong. Gang conduct and gang mores are ever more widely known. Bad conduct by a small group infects a spreading circle. This is the danger which underlies the tragedy of the bopping gangs in Red Hook or the Bronx. The destructive effects are not limited to the youngsters directly involved.

If you sample the upper-income suburbs of any eastern metropolis you quickly find telltale indications of gang mores among "respectable children." These are children of parents who are deeply shocked when they read of teen-age knifings in the New York slums. These are the parents who never suspect that Tommy and Irene are anything but, perhaps, "a little wild."

"I don't know what kids are coming to these days," they tell their neighbors. "Take that Tommy of mine. He wants the car every night. Why, the other evening it was three in the morning when he got in. When I asked him where he had been he said it was none of my business."

Underlying this talk is the firm assumption that there is nothing wrong with Tommy. Of course, he has been having a little trouble with his third year high school studies. But what do you expect. It's hard to get kids to buckle down to their lessons these days. They do not know that Tommy is spending most of his evenings with a bunch of teen-agers at the Pizza Palace on the County Road. They do not know that the favorite dare of these youngsters is to drink an upended pint of whiskey without stopping for breath—and then get behind the wheel of their father's car. They do not know that several boys in this group smoke reefers. These parents chatter over the cocktails at the country club about the "Anti-Virgin Club," which that newspaper reported up in Canada someplace. Thank God, they sigh, fifteen-year-old Irene "isn't like that." They don't know that Irene lost her virginity with one of Tommy's boy friends in the back seat of the family car last summer. They don't know that in Tommy's gang Irene is rated as a pushover.

It is much more comfortable to think of teen-age delinquency as something which flowers in the deep slums of New York and Chicago and Philadelphia and Los Angeles. The sad and dangerous truth, as I had found, is that the slums are only reservoirs and, perhaps, tradition setters for antisocial adolescent conduct at all social levels. Poverty increases the pressures which drive young people into blind revolt against the world. But it is not the cause of the revolt. Delinquency is a symptom, not a disease, and the disease knows no geographical and no social boundaries.

Youngsters caught by delinquency think there is no cure for it. "It's the way the world is," they told me time and again. "Always going to be gangs. Always going to be fighting. Nobody's going to stop it."

This, I am certain, is where they are wrong. It can be stopped and it has been stopped. The disease which produces delinquency can be cured. We have the methods and the remedies, but the cure is not an easy one with an ailment so complex and deep-rooted.

The way to begin the attack, of course, is to take a close and careful look at the shook-up generation and how it behaves. What, after all, is the gang and what is its life?

2

the gang

THE first gang with which I got acquainted was the Cobras. None of the Cobras knows how or when the gang was started. The Cobras are an active "bopping" or street-fighting club which has its base in one of the older Brooklyn housing projects.

As far as the Cobras know, the gang was there when they began to grow up in the neighborhood or when they moved there from Manhattan or from out of town. As far as they know the gang has always been there. No Cobra can imagine his world, or any world, without a street gang. His world is a narrow one. Gang life fills it almost completely.

You can meet the Cobras any day of the week from four o'clock on in the afternoon. That is the hour when they begin to collect outside Schroeder's candy store, just across the street from the Whitman Housing Project. Winter, spring or summer you will see them in this same spot at this same hour doing the same thing—teetering back and forth, heel-to-toe, slightly loose-jointed, shoulders hunched a little, hands deep thrust in trousers' pockets, heads and chins bobbing and darting, duckfashion, eyes quick to detect any stranger moving down the street.

The Cobras are protecting their demesne—"minding our

turf," in the argot of the streets. With a little time out for dinner some of them will stand on that corner until 11 P.M. of a winter's night, regardless of cold, and until 1 or 2 A.M. (unless chased away by the police) on sultry summer evenings.

"Minding our turf" is the main preoccupation of the Cobras. They live a life which touches the ordinary adult world only along the edges. Theirs is a subculture, a subsociety with its own mores, codes, ceremonies, language and interests. The Cobras do not know what goes on in the other world. nor do they care. If in some respects their way of life seemed to me to provide a grotesquerie of the adult world of nations, only a few more perceptive members possess the insight to comprehend this. For the most part the Cobras live within an impenetrable shell of their own. Theirs is a world of young people harshly buffeted by grim realities—poverty, hunger, physical hardship, danger, displacement, disease and deprivation. Beset by force and violence they escape into paranoid visions of grandeur, daydreams of demonic power, ecstasies of sadism, endless fantasies with a gun. They erect a bizarre construction, half real, half delusionary. Within this structure they make a last-ditch stand against adult pressures and conflict beyond their immature powers to cope with or comprehend.

Here is the street gang in its most vicious flowering. Most youngsters in America, I know, do not face the struggle for survival which confronts the Cobras and strongly shapes their mores and their conduct. But the pattern of antisocial activity set by gangs like the Cobras casts a dark shadow over an ever-widening area of the nation—good neighborhoods and bad, small cities and large, New York, San Francisco and Chicago. What the Cobras do today shook-up high school seniors in Great Neck, Long Island, or Beverly Hills, California, will consciously or unconsciously imitate and reflect tomorrow.

Most of the Cobras happen to be Negro. They live, play, work and fight beside and in close relation with a "brother

club," the Silver Arrows, whose membership is largely Puerto
Rican. The racial divisions closely follow those of the population of the Whitman Housing Project. Geography rather
than ethnic differences usually determines gang composition.
"Integrated" gangs are not uncommon. Most gangs include
at least a few minority race members. The Cobras and the
Arrows are "tight" in the language of the street. This means
that they are close allies in the treacherous, shifting sphere
of the bop. The Cobras and the Arrows have many enemies.
When they look beyond the boundaries of the Whitman
project they see a dark and dangerous jungle populated by
unknown hordes which may strike at any moment.

"You can be sure I never cross Gowanus Parkway without
my piece [gun]," Chico told me. His comrades nodded sagely.
"You don't know when you might meet somebody who has
seen you before. Or somebody who hasn't seen you before,"
one added.

Within this sea of danger exist two well-known, well-
identified enemies—the Rovers (Irish-Italian) and the
Apaches (largely Irish), two street gangs on the perimeters
of the Whitman project. The conflict between the Cobras
and the Arrows, on the one hand, and the Rovers and
Apaches on the other has roots so twisted that none of the
teen-agers can tell the story straight. The enmity is as deep,
bitter and tortuous as any feud in Montenegro. This spring
of ever-replenishing hatred conditions the violent antisocial
nature of the activity of all four clubs.

The Cobras divide themselves into two categories—Big
People and Little People. This division is common to most
Negro street gangs. Big People are sixteen to nineteen, for
the most part. They are the core of the fighting gang. Little
People are younger, ranging from nine or ten to about fifteen.
The ages are approximate. There are fourteen-year-olds
among the Big People. And occasionally a twenty-year-old
will be found among Little People. In predominantly white

gangs the divisions often are more elaborate—diapers (8-11), midgets (10-13), juniors (12-15) and seniors (15-20).

The Cobras are what social workers call a "structured" gang. That is, they have a leadership clique with titles, offices and responsibilities—a President (public policy, domestic and foreign relations, strategy), a Vice-President (Chief of Staff and Second in Command), a War Counselor (war plans, intelligence, tactics) and a Gunsmith or Armorer (weapons and logistics). The Little People have a similar top echelon but are subordinate to over-all control by the Big People.

Members of the Cobras told me that they "elect" their President. They also told me that they "vote" on decisions. Actually, there is not much democracy. It is more like a South American junta. The clique which runs the Little People generally succeeds to leadership of the Big People when age and circumstances produce a change in gang leadership.

This happens every two or three years. Arrests, casualties and desertion caused by jobs or marriage accomplish this.

The present leaders of the Cobras came to power in the summer of 1957. They had been Little People until violent tragedy made them Big People overnight. One midsummer evening the older gang members boarded a subway train, heading for downtown Brooklyn. They had been drinking heavily and started to "sound" (insult) the passengers. A trainman intervened. They wounded him badly with their switchblades and threw him off the train at the next station. Police corralled the whole group. Most were convicted and sent up for long terms in state institutions.

The Little People inherited the gang. Their first act was to change its name. The club had been called the Royal Imperials. Some years before it went under the title of the Huns. Now, the old name had acquired too much notoriety with the police. It had to be changed as a matter of defensive necessity. The members decided to call themselves Cobras because the name sounded tough. Terror value rates high

in gang nomenclature. That is why there are Scorpions, Dragons (a great favorite), Vikings, Jaguars, Warriors, Huns, Demons, Comanches, Hellbenders, Sioux (pronounced Cy-ox), Tigers, Villains, Cherokees, Daggers, Stonekillers and Stompers on the streets of New York. Status value is another attribute as indicated by clubs calling themselves Viceroys, Lords, Egyptian Kings, Royal Niles, Centurians, Crusaders, Dukes, and Gents. Bloody victories in street combat have lent aura to the curiously named Bishops, Chaplains, Enchanters and Sportsmen. Probably no one will ever know why some gangs call themselves the Tims, the Jits, the Baldies or the Pigtown Lords.

When I asked a Cobra the purpose of his organization he told me that it is a social club made up of friends and good fellows. "We are," he said, "all for one and one for all." In case of danger the club provides protection and self-defense.

Protection against what? Protection of the Cobra members and their turf against any threat from the outside. The Cobra does not regard himself as a menace to anyone. But the world seems to him to be filled with menace. There is only one small island of comparative safety—his turf. On his own turf and in the presence of his own comrades he feels relatively, but only relatively, secure. Twenty-two-year-old Trigger now lives an hour's subway ride from Whitman Houses. But he comes down almost every night to be with the gang. "Man, I just don't feel safe up there in the Bronx," he says.

The Cobra does not know much about the geography of the United States. He may not even know how to get from Brooklyn to Manhattan. But there is one bit of geography which he can walk blindfold. This is his turf, the demesne the Cobras call their own. The Cobras share their demesne with the Silver Arrows. It is bounded by the limits of the housing project and is, actually, an enclave. In times of a rumble this has certain advantages (interior lines, ease of concentration for defense). But it also has grave disadvan-

tages. Any Cobra who must leave the project for school or work is forced to walk right into enemy territory.

The boundary of the Cobra island is defined as precisely as a surveyor's map. On one perimeter, for example, the Cobra's demesne extends across the street from the Houses to include a half block occupied by a store-front church, a liquor store, a shoe repair shop, Schroeder's candy store and a bar-and-grill. On another periphery, however, the line stops at the edge of the project. The street and commercial establishments fronting the boundary are no man's land— safe enough during a "cool" but fighting ground during a rumble, an uncertain area where one side or another may at any sudden moment "jap" an unwary alien.

Security is a constant worry of the Cobras. Each has his nickname or *nom de guerre*. This is designed to prevent enemies (police, parole officers, rival gangs) from penetrating real identities and tracing participants in rumbles. But the nicknames are chosen, as well, for prowess value. Favorite *noms de gang* include Blood, Snake, Leadpipe, China, Knobby, Hatchet, Killer, Geronimo, Cochise, Diablo, Rocky, Moto, Johnny the Bop, Vice, Dice, Goat, Savage, Wolf and Saint.

Perhaps the name with the greatest status value is Kemo. Kemo was the name of a famous character in a radio serial of the late thirties. Street gang tradition has it that Kemo was the name used by one of the greatest bops in gang history— a little man, unimpressive physically, but "the fastest man in the world with a knife." Zorro, another radio and television name, is rapidly rising in popularity and status.

There are forty to fifty Cobras in all, roughly divided between Big People and Little People. About two-thirds of them are enrolled in school but many are irregular in attendance. Half of the others have jobs. Half do not.

Monk is a member of the Cobras. He is fifteen. His father died when he was three years old. His mother is a cleaning woman. She leaves the apartment a little after seven in the morning. Before she goes she tells Monk to get up. Monk does not get up. He is supposed to be in school at eight-thirty but more often than not he skips school. It is almost ten before he drags out of bed. He cooks some French fries on the gas stove. This is breakfast. Two or three times a week this is his only meal of the day. His mother has left him twenty-five cents for lunch on the dresser. He takes the twenty-five cents and wanders down to the street.

On the corner he finds Chico, who is about his age and also a truant. With Chico is Dice, seventeen, and possessor of a part-time job. Dice has twenty-five cents. Monk and Dice pool this money and get an old wino to buy them a bottle of sneaky pete (cheap wine) for thirty-nine cents. They are too young to make the purchase themselves. They give the wino a drink and down the rest. This puts them into a haze of well-being for a couple of hours. In the afternoon they scare up the price of another bottle of cheap wine. But by 4 P.M. the glow of the wine has long since worn off. Monk and his friends feel bored, mean, depressed and hungry. None of them has eaten all day. They are spoiling for trouble and trouble usually accommodates them.

If the fundamental concept of the Cobras is demesne and its protection, their basic mystique is "heart." Heart is what passes on the street for bravery. Smokey is the leader of the Cobras because of heart. Chico is a respected club member because of heart. Blood, the war counselor, won his post through heart.

So central is this mystique that it comprises the device of the most notorious of all the bopping gangs of New York, the Chaplains. Their motto is "All Chaplains have heart."

Heart as defined by the bopping clubs is not the exact equivalent of courage as, say, Richard Coeur de Lion understood it. For, while curious medieval anachronisms do exist in the bopping world the parallels do not always hold true.

"Heart, well, that's when a bop isn't afraid of anything or anybody," Dice tells you. "He will do absolutely anything. When the chips are down—if he has to fight five he'll fight five. He'll say, 'I'm the butcher, man. I'm the hatchet. If you need anyone to pull the trigger I'll pull the trigger.'

"You take Chico," Dice says. "He has more heart than anyone I ever saw. He's crazy, that boy. Been up to Warwick three times. He don't care what he do. Once we had a rumble with the Chaplains. You know what he did? He went out alone right into Chaplains' turf. In daylight. Just walked in, inviting them to jap him, hoping they would jap him. He'll fight anybody. No matter how many they are. That Chico— he stays drunk all the time. Isn't ever sober. But, man, he sure have heart."

Heart, as the bop defines it, is audacity, devil-may-care disregard for self and consequences. Heart is fourteen-year-old Snake walking up to a patrolman on the corner and making a grab for his pistol. Heart is sixteen-year-old Rocky waiting in ambush outside a school and firing a rifle into a group of teen-agers as they come out, joking and unaware of danger. Heart is Dice taking a dare to jump down three flights of stairs (and only prevented from carrying it out when someone grabs his legs as he leaps).

A boy shows heart by laughing at his attackers when he is japped outside his neighborhood. He shows heart by sounding a street boy bigger and tougher than himself.

The opposite of heart is punking out. When a cool has been on for some time gang leaders may order a "shin fight" (sham battle) between the Little People and the Big People. The shin fight simulates gang combat except that knives and guns are not used and blows are not supposed to be struck below the belt or in the face. A shin battle tests heart and shows which boys will be the most vicious and daring street fighters.

Heart is not the sole criterion for gang leadership. Gang

leaders must also have intelligence, insight and knowledge
of the world surpassing that of their comrades. Otherwise,
the gang will be led into suicidal encounters with larger
and more powerful street enemies. It will embark on ven-
tures which bring on fatal encounters with the police.

Smokey, leader of the Cobras, has heart. But he also has
more brains than his comrades. The same is true of Vincent,
leader of the Silver Arrows. But the leaders of the Apaches
are another case. The Apaches are a gang nearing the stage
of final dissolution. They are two or three years older than
the Cobras or the Arrows. Once they were all-powerful in the
neighborhood but that was several years back.

One by one the Apaches left Whitman project. In part this
was because of the influx of Negro and Puerto Rican families
but mostly it was the product of the violence of the street
club. They got into trouble with housing authorities, social
workers and the police. Many were expelled from the project
and moved into nearby cold-water flats. Conflict between the
Apaches and the gangs in the project grew more savage.

"Sometimes," a social worker said, "it seemed as though
the Apaches knew in their subconscious that they were bound
to lose. After each battle they grew more wild. They were
determined to go down in a blaze of violence."

So destructive were the Apaches even when not on the warpath that they were barred from the Neighborhood Center
and then from the Catholic Youth Center. Each rebuff stimu-
lated the leaders to new outrages. A street-club worker was
assigned to the group, but one evening half a dozen Apaches
attacked the man as he stood in friendly conversation with
them on a busy street corner. He was sent to the hospital with
serious knife wounds. Although they could now muster only
a third of the strength of the Cobras and Arrows they deliberately provoked battles in which they inevitably lost more
strength. Finally, a dozen Apaches were arrested on charges
of possession of concealed weapons. The gang survives but

only as a crippled remnant. Obviously its days are numbered.

Such suicidal drives have been observed in many other gangs. A certain vicious East Harlem gang has suffered an annihilating crisis each year for the past five. The gang's leadership is provided by boys from one large, disorderly family. When one brother leads the gang into a debacle (involving a gun battle with police, a fatal knifing or some other major crime) the next oldest boy succeeds to gang leadership and starts out again with a group of slightly younger boys. The gang is kept alive by the father of the boy leaders. He trains his sons in gang fighting and encourages them to act out his own aggressions by propelling them into wild bouts with the social order.

Hugh Johnson of the New York City Youth Board has spent ten years in close observation of street gangs. He believes their leadership follows a fairly definite cycle.

In the first stage there is quite normal adolescent leadership with few pathological tendencies. As conflict sharpens, the gangs push forward a new type of leader—the deeply disturbed, homicidal individual. Such youngsters usually come to a quick, inglorious end and drag the gang down with them. Then comes a more controlled cool "organization man," who dictates gang policy and gives members little voice.

Now, with the spread of gangs and gang conduct they are attracting many youngsters who would not normally join street groups—very shook-up youngsters, treatment failures from state institutions, narcotics users and even neighborhood boys from better families who previously were immune to the attraction of the gang.

Of the new recruits the narcotics addicts offer the greatest problem. They are not good street fighters although under the influence of drugs they may shoot and stab in a completely aberrational way. But they make a definite contribution to the gang. They are much more intelligent and creative than the ordinary teen-ager. Their role becomes that of imaginative advisers to the gang leaders. They are distinguished for the perverseness and sadism of the tactics and schemes which they put forward.

The structure of the Rovers differs a good deal from that of the Cobras. They have no ritual. Indeed, they deny that they are a street club. No one will admit that he is a leader. It is only when they "go down" or embark on a rumble that the gang structure can be clearly identified. In combat the Rovers act precisely the way their fellow street adolescents do.

But there are differences. One is in style. The Cobras dress like "real diddley bops"—first-class street fighters. Take Blood, the Cobras' war counselor. He has a job and his first week's pay went to buy a twenty-dollar gray alpine-style hat with narrow brim. The hat is decorated with a thick braided gray cord and a neat gray and blue feather. Blood calls this hat a "stenjer." The name derives from the fact that the hat has a "stingy" rather than a "generous" brim.

Blood wears a navy-blue gabardine half coat, peg-top trousers, white and blue longitudinally striped nylon socks, thin-soled black shoes with white-piped welts.

Jimmy, another Cobra with a job, sports a light beige topcoat with black velvet collar. He wears a tight blue beret, silk or dacron shirts, horizontally striped orange-and-black jacket which comes almost to his knees, narrow trousers and thin-soled black woven-leather pumps. He usually displays a large brilliant attached to a fine gold wire in the lobe of his left ear.

Blood and Jimmy dress in what Brooklyn gangs regard as high fashion. However, Central Harlem and lower East Side gang members have abandoned flashy costumes. The Central Harlem youngster has turned to gray flannel suits, regimentally striped neckties, well-cut Harris tweed jackets. He has gone Ivy League with a vengeance. His clothes are cut in Brooks Brothers pattern. Leaders often sport tightly rolled umbrellas with gold gooseneck handles. They have everything but a Madison Avenue brown leather attaché case in which to carry their zip guns. These youngsters seek to create the image of a "cool, cultured, beat-the-rap" type.

The difference in costume between Brooklyn and Manhattan, in the opinion of one observer, represents a cultural lag.

"Brooklyn is about four years behind Manhattan," this man said. "Bedford-Stuyvesant is four years behind Harlem and Williamsburg is four years behind that. Confidentially, Brooklyn is out of this world."

The Rovers display no special peculiarities of every-day dress. They effect the sports shirts and salt-and-pepper odd coats and slacks which are the convention of the high school adolescent throughout the country. Some favor butch haircuts. Others the Sal Mineo spit lock plastered to the forehead. Many wear sideburns long and display ragged Tarzan back bobs in imitation of their beloved Elvis.

But, regardless of style, a street club member is recognizable at a glance by other members of shook-up society.

How this is accomplished is not easy to put down in words. But anyone who has spent much time with teen-age street fighters can spot them at a glance. The gang youngster, whether in his own neighborhood or out, always has a wary eye for enemies. He never feels secure and he betrays this insecurity with quick, darting looks, the stolen glance over the shoulder, the nervous movement of hands (usually held close to the concealed switchblade or zip gun), the almost compulsive twitch of his body. All of these are telltales to other gang members.

The argot in which the youngsters speak is another recognition factor. The argot seems to derive from the world of bebop, jitterbugging and jazz. The street adolescents employ much of the vocabulary of hot music but usually give the words a different connotation. There are no variations in street argot between adolescents of different ethnic background. "They all know the sound," a street club worker said.

Their conversations may not be readily understood by persons unfamiliar with the shook-up generation. When a strange boy walks past the Cobra candy store the following conversation may ensue:

"Who you swinging with, man?"

"Why, I'm swinging with the Bishops, man."

"Good, man. We're tight with the Bishops. We're a brother club. How about dropping a dime, man, and we'll get a bottle of sneaky pete."

"Okay, man. I thought you might be shaking me down."

"Oh, you figured you might have to shuffle, eh?"

"That's what I thought, man. But I'm telling you I got a piece on me. Nobody going to jap me, man."

"I thought you might be a coolie, man."

"You trying to sound me? Let's get that sneaky pete and have us a gig."

Or, in English:

"What street club do you belong to?"

"I belong to the Bishops."

"Good, we're friendly with the Bishops. They are affiliated with our club. How about contributing a dime toward a bottle of wine?"

"Okay, I was afraid you would try to hold me up."

"You thought you might have to fight?"

"Yes, that's why I'm carrying a gun. I'm not letting anyone take me by surprise."

"I thought you might not belong to a gang."

"Don't kid me. Let's get that wine and have a party."

The concept of the coolie is common to all the street gangs. The coolie is a boy who does not belong to a street club. He may be a quiet, retiring youngster who pays a daily tribute of ten cents or a quarter to a gang member who protects him from attack by other teen-agers. Or he may be an out-standing boy in the neighborhood, good in sports, good in school, well liked by other youngsters, who simply stands aside from street activity. Such a boy often is respected and not interfered with by boys dedicated to the bop. Such youngsters can live in a community dominated by street conflict and be untouched by it. In unusual cases they may even be regarded as part of the gang but are tacitly excused from combat.

Much more frequent is the youngster who is "drafted" into the gang. The draft is used by all four gangs in the neighborhood of Whitman Houses—the Cobras, the Arrows, the Rovers and the Apaches.

Smokey, leader of the Cobras, frankly admits that the draft is the only way in which he can maintain his order of battle at full strength.

"There has to be a draft," he says. "There doesn't seem to be any real place in the world for the coolie."

Smokey is unaware how close his remark comes to paralleling those of statesmen pondering the disappearance of national neutrality in the world struggle of great powers.

Application of the draft is very simple. A recruiting squad of three or four boys approaches a coolie.

"Do you want to join the club or do you want a punch in the belly?" they ask. Sometimes, they knock the boy down first and then ask him, just to show they mean business. Few boys refuse to join. If a draftee tries to duck a rumble he is likely to earn new beatings for punking out. Sometimes the beating is inflicted by a formal punishment squad of half a dozen boys. They make the offender run a gantlet while they beat him savagely with brass-studded garrison belts or baseball bats. The next time he goes along on the rumble.

The Cobras have never kicked a member out of the gang although boys have been punished for desertion. It is rare for a boy to be expelled but it sometimes happens when a boy's conduct is so irrational that he repeatedly endangers his fellow members. But since all of the gang are shook-up or disturbed they tolerate much before moving against a comrade.

If a boy is found club hopping (changing sides) or cheesy (guilty of treason) he is in danger of death. If the gang gets its hands on such a boy it will beat him to death or come close to it.

The gang code on treason carries an important escape clause. It is not treason if a member tells something to a street club worker. If a street club worker orders a boy to hand over his zip gun the boy will comply. This is not a violation of gang code. If a street club worker learns of a rumble from a gang member and thwarts the projected fight this is not treason, either. Nor is a gang regarded as punking out if it runs away from the police when they appear on the scene of a planned rumble.

The status of the street club worker is something like that of an International Red Cross representative on the world battlefields. His neutrality and good intentions are recognized by unwritten gang law. No harm accrues to gang members because of contact with him. Intervention of the police is regarded as *force majeure* and thus beyond the control of gang members. Intervention which enables a gang to avoid combat without loss of "rep," or reputation, is secretly welcomed by most boys.

Gangs spend only a small part of their time fighting. They hang about the street corners for weeks doing nothing. Boredom is acute. They do not stand alone, of course. Each gang has its following of girls. In some cases they are organized into ladies' auxiliaries—usually called "debs." Sometimes, the debs constitute a fighting gang which engages in combat with other girl gangs.

The Cobras used to have a debs unit called the "Cobrettes." It was led by a blue-eyed, blond-haired girl named Lulu.

She was fourteen years old, five feet two and looked like an angel in black leather jacket and faded blue jeans. She carried a switchblade knife and bossed her gang like a top sergeant. Somehow, Lulu lost interest in bopping about a year ago. Perhaps it is the quiet boy she now goes steady with. At any rate the Cobrettes no longer are a fighting group. They hide weapons for the Cobras and stir up a good deal of the trouble which the Cobras get into. But they do not go on rumbles themselves.

Rose is a Cobra deb. She is a mature fifteen, with snapping black eyes, black hair and tan skin. When trouble is brewing between the Cobras and Rovers she likes to say with relish: "Let's go down! I'm going to get me a guinea!" She may not realize that she is echoing the remarks of Judy, the girl friend of Tony, a leader of the Rovers. "C'mon, Tony," Judy says, "let's get us one of those nigger bastards!"

Not infrequently it is the Roses and Judys who start the rumble by reporting insults, real or imaginary, inflicted by the enemy gang.

Not many Cobras go steady. They do not have time. A steady girl makes demands that divert them from their main occupation—the gang.

"You go steady," Chocolate says, "and first thing she wants you to spend all your time with her. She wants you to stop fighting. She's afraid you get hurt. She starts talking that marriage stuff. None of that going steady for me."

Not that gang members lead a monastic life. On the contrary. "These boys have no sex problem," a street worker said. "At least not like the middle-class kids. Some of the ways they have of satisfying themselves are shocking. But frustration is not their problem."

The Cobras classify girls into three categories—plain lays, in-betweens and debs. Their attitude toward a "lay" is that she exists simply to satisfy primitive sexual needs. They treat such girls with sadistic contempt. The in-betweens get vary-

ing treatment as the name suggests. The boys hold debs
in higher regard. They are alert to revenge insults against
these girls and will fight an outside boy who tries to date
a deb.

They brag of their sexual prowess with all three classes
of girls. They are proud rather than disturbed when they
impregnate a girl. This proves manly virility. Boys boast of
"my son" or "my daughter" begotten with a teen-age partner.
But they offer nothing to the support of the child and
marry the girl only when confronted with the alternative
of a charge of statutory rape. The boys employ contraceptives
with reluctance—usually only when the girl insists. They tell
a girl she is no good if she insists on a contraceptive. Often,
a boy secretly pricks the contraceptive with a pin before
using it.

"This will give Dee-Dee a surprise," the boy boasts to
his pals.

Perversions, particularly group sexual activities, are frequent. The "line-up" is a standard part of street life. Boys
often "con" a girl into having intercourse, then, regardless
of her protests, invite half a dozen other adolescents to share
her.

The "circle jerk," or mass masturbation, is a common sex
activity. Groups of as many as twenty Rovers join in such
a ritual on a summer evening in a deserted public park.
Sometimes, a boy and girl may give an exhibition in the
center of the circle while group masturbation goes on.

Last winter, a group of Rovers maintained a teen-age
prostitute in their exclusive possession for a couple of months.
They picked up the girl (who was only sixteen) in a bar-and-
grill. When they found she was suffering from gonorrhea
they took her to a doctor for treatment. After she was pronounced cured they began to use her as a group prostitute.
By one trick and another they managed to keep her in their

own homes for weeks before their parents realized what was happening.

The world of the street gang is a male-dominant world. The boys do pretty much as they like with the girls. If a girl resists their desires they drop her. There are always more pliable girls at hand.

The favorite dance in the neighborhood centers and candy stores is the "fish" or the grind. The fish is a slow, quiet hip movement resembling a burlesque house grind. As one social worker says: "Let's be honest—the fish is nothing but a dry run." It is danced body-to-body with hardly any movement of the feet. Because it is nothing but a sexual exercise some centers try to ban it. But when the director turns his back the youngsters move together again and grind away.

This does not mean that Puerto Rican youngsters have abandoned the cha-cha and the merengue. Nor that white adolescents have given up rock 'n' roll. But the trend is to the fish.

Drink is the curse of the shook-up kids. With few exceptions boys and girls drink from the age of eleven or twelve. They drink wine—sneaky pete, so called because it sneaks up behind and hits you when you don't expect it. Or thunderbird (a slightly more expensive wine) or half-and-half (half wine, half whiskey). They drink anything put before them. But since they have little money they concentrate on wine.

Like all youngsters they enjoy dances and parties. But long before the evening is over most of the boys are drunk and many of the girls have been sick in the ill-smelling toilets. It is not uncommon for boys to sneak a bottle into school and snatch pulls at it all day long.

Even worse than drink is dope—pot or tea. There are few gangs in which no member uses drugs. The Arrows have a rule forbidding members to use dope. They also have a rule forbidding debs to drink. But this is unusual.

It is safe to say that there is a "pusher" or dope salesman within calling distance of the hangouts of every street gang in New York City. This is not accidental. Shook-up youngsters are excellent prospects for dope. Dope salesmen are like any enterprising businessmen. They hunt out the potential buyer.

"Try a reefer," one boy tells another. "Go ahead. I dare you. Don't be chicken."

Unless the boy wants to punk out he tries the marijuana. Next time it is cocaine or heroin. "Go ahead. Try it. Just for kicks."

There's not a teen-age street kid in New York who doesn't know another youngster who takes dope occasionally. And most of them know who sells the dope. So do the people who live in the neighborhoods. Why don't the police or the federal men halt dope sales and arrest the salesmen, the big businessmen who profit by the trade? This is a question a good many thoughtful citizens would like to have answered.

Most youngsters belonging to the seventy-five or one hundred active street fighting gangs in New York City come from lower-income classes. Many are the products of impoverished cultural backgrounds, the plantation economy of South Carolina or the overpopulated areas of Puerto Rico. But not all by any means. Not a few Rovers and Apaches stem from middle-income families. Regardless of economic or cultural differences the similarity in delinquency patterns throughout the country is striking.

The greatest contrast between the Cobras of Brooklyn and the Sportsmen of Jamaica, Long Island, for instance, is technological. The Jamaica boys have access to cars. Theirs is a mobile existence. They hang out not at a neighborhood candy store but at an ice-cream stand out on the highway. In terms of geography their horizon is much wider. They are not confined to a constricted slum area deep within a crowded city.

But geographical freedom does not broaden their ethos. They know the "sound." Their conduct is molded in the same narrow, aggressive antisocial patterns. Their interests outside their own adolescent world are no broader than those of the Cobras. They, too, dream fantasies with a gun. They, too, build their lives on conflict and hostility to other groups and individuals. If their rituals are outwardly more sophisticated they have the same inner emptiness. They judge by the same false standards of "heart" and "punking out." Instead of testing courage in a shin battle they sometimes play "chicken"—the suicidal game in which two drivers race their cars head-on at each other—sixty, seventy, eighty miles an hour. The first to turn aside is chicken—a coward and despised. They treat one another with the same brutal sadism as the Cobras or the Rovers. They live in the same revolt against forces they do not understand. They are in the same sense shook-up.

The cousins of the Jamaica Sportsmen are to be found in Lake Forest, Illinois, or Long Beach, California, or Denver, Colorado. There are, of course, different degrees of being shook-up and regional peculiarities of conduct. In the culturally deprived ghettos of New York the name of the gang and its "rep" may acquire special aura. It may, indeed, serve as a substitute for many things which are lacking in the lives of its members. It may provide a reason for existence, a source of personal satisfaction, a pseudo-purpose for a life which lacks any purpose.

In the gang the street boy feels himself important. Nowhere else does he seem to matter. Not at home (if he has what can be called a home). Not at school, where he can barely read, where there is nothing he can do well enough to give him even a faint glow of achievement. Not on the job, where the boss makes him feel inadequate and inferior.

But with his comrades in his gang he is important. He is needed. He is wanted. He has a place. His gang is his life.

As it grows in rep so he grows in rep. He stands taller on the streets. He shows his heart with more reckless abandon. He becomes a Big Man.

There is no essential difference between Chico and Charley. Chico was born in Puerto Rico, brought to the United States by his mother at the age of nine, raised fatherless in the street-fighting grounds of Brooklyn. Charley, son of moderately well-to-do parents in Philadelphia, brought to Stamford, Connecticut, by his mother after the divorce, was raised in the suburbs of New York.

Chico can hardly read. He doesn't speak English well. He seldom is home. The only place he feels that he belongs is with the Cobras. He drinks every day. His pride is that no one has as much heart as he. He will do anything to show this. Actually, Chico is suicidal. He doesn't care what happens to him. Not after a few drinks.

Charley doesn't read well, either. He reads the comics—the horror comics. Not much else. He hates the home where his mother seldom is and his father never. He drinks every day. The only time he feels himself is with the crowd at the ice-cream joint. His pride is that no one can chicken him on the highway. Actually, Charley is suicidal. He doesn't really care what happens to him. Not after a few drinks.

Chico and Charley are shook-up products of a shook-up world. A world of violence, some of it self-created, some of it not. A world of antagonism and aggression. A world of conflict. A world from which there is no real escape, for, as one of them put it, "A Bishop is always a Bishop, and a Chaplain is always a Chaplain, and there is no such thing as a cool."

3

the rumble

ONE hot August night the Cobras were standing outside Schroeder's candy store. Smokey, the leader, was there. So was Blood, his war counselor, Hawk, a thin gangling boy of great instability, and many others. Across the street in a small plaza of the Whitman Housing Project, Vincent, the leader of the Silver Arrows, and several of his gang were teasing some girls. It was sultry and quiet. In the distance there was an occasional flicker of heat lightning. Later it would rain. It was an evening like a hundred summer evenings on the streets of New York.

"Nothing was going on that night and that's a fact," Smokey recalls. "It was too hot to do anything. We didn't have any plans. We were just passing the time, when some of my friends came by."

Smokey's friends were leaders of the Bishops and the Stompers, two bopping gangs with which the Cobras are allied. The Bishops' turf lies a couple of miles away, near downtown Brooklyn. The Stompers' base is Bedford-Stuyvesant.

"We hear you been having a little trouble around here," the Bishops' president said to Smokey.

This was true, Smokey said. The Cobras and Arrows were

in a state of constant feud with the Rovers and Apaches who lived outside the housing project. All summer long there had been skirmishes.

As one Rover put it: "Every year it is the same thing. All quiet until the church bazaar. Then, the project boys come down. Before the bazaar is over the trouble starts. There is nothing Father Mullen can do about it. Something is just bound to happen."

The church fete is held in June. This year a Cobra was japped as he walked back home from the bazaar. He was badly beaten. In retaliation the Cobras jumped three Rovers as they passed through the project the next night. Sporadic raids followed. A serious one had occurred the previous week. Three carloads of Rovers roared into the housing project. They drove their automobiles onto the sidewalk and plowed through a group of youngsters under a street light. Two boys were taken to the hospital. Several others were hurt.

This was the "little trouble" to which the Bishop chief referred. If Smokey wanted revenge the Bishops would help out. They had taken the precaution of ordering action squads to join them within half an hour.

The opportunity was too good to miss. Smokey consulted his ally, Vincent. It was agreed to "go down" on the Rovers as soon as the main body of fifty Bishops and Stompers arrived.

Usually it was the duty of Blood, as the war counselor, to develop a careful campaign plan when the Cobras proposed to go on the offensive. But tonight Smokey decided on a surprise. The Rovers' turf comprises an area about a quarter of a mile square only three blocks from the housing project. Nine o'clock in the evening was fixed for H-Hour. At that time the Rovers would be congregated around three candy stores on Beaver Street, only a few doors apart. Because of the heat they would be standing on the sidewalks with the jukeboxes in the stores blaring at full volume. In their light sports shirts and khaki pants few of them would be armed.

The Bishops and Stompers had two cars—something neither the Cobras nor Arrows possessed. The cars would drive down Beaver Street, firing at random. While attention was diverted the boys on foot would infiltrate the side streets and try to come up on the Rovers from behind.

Blood wanted to send two or three snakes (spies or intelligence agents) to check the location and strength of the Rovers. Smokey vetoed that. There wasn't time. In twenty minutes the main body of the brother clubs would arrive. They must be ready to go down before the Rovers detected any strangers in the neighborhood.

Cannon, gunsmith for the Cobras, disappeared with two of the Little People. They went to get the principal armament of the Cobras—two Mauser pistols, four machetes, a shotgun with the barrel sawed off, and a .22 caliber Winchester repeating rifle. Other boys slipped away to retrieve zip guns and switchblades from caches around the project. Some weapons were being held by girl friends. Others were hidden in the bushes, quickly available in case of need.

At a little after nine the gangs were ready. The Cobras and Arrows had their weapons, a bottle had been passed around and the Bishops and Stompers were arriving in twos and threes. Larger groups might have attracted the attention of police. They did not congregate on the street corner but dispersed in small knots and moved toward the Rovers' turf. As they slipped through the drowsy streets some boys snapped radio aerials off parked cars. The aerials are a deadly weapon. Wielded as a steel whip they can lay a face open to the bone. Used as a spear they will penetrate the lungs or stomach.

As the Cobras neared Beaver Street they could hear the wail of the jukeboxes. In the distance thunder reverberated. Suddenly came a ragged fusillade of shots and the roar of motors. The rumble was on. The cars raced to the end of Beaver Street, spun on whining tires and whirled back for a second pass at the stunned Rovers. Glass shattered as shots broke store-front windows. The Cobras, Bishops, Arrows and Stompers poured from the side streets and swarmed on the three candy stores. This was not a "fair one." Four and five youngsters jumped on each of the Rovers, beating the boys to the ground, stabbing with knives, flailing with steel rods, stomping with their boots. Beaver Street was a turmoil of shouts, cries for help, screams of pain. There was a thin plink from a zip gun and the solid blast of the sawed-off shotgun. Then, in the distance came the moan of a police siren.

As suddenly as they had descended the Cobras and their allies fled down the alleys toward the project. By the time the squad cars braked to a halt the attackers had vanished. The first drops of the delayed thunderstorm began to patter down on the pavement, now empty except for three wounded boys who still lay there groaning in agony.

Five Rovers were badly injured in this battle. The life of Ricky, a leader, hung in the balance for days. He survived but lost a lung. It had been ripped to shreds with knife stabs. Months later he reappeared in the candy stores, pale, thin, tight-lipped with hatred. The police arrested half a dozen Cobras. Finally, all were released except Hawk, who was charged with the frantic slashing of Ricky. Nearly a year later he was still being held for trial.*

And a year later the bitterness engendered by the rumble had not been dissipated. A "cool" was negotiated by street club workers. But it was an uneasy truce, often broken. For months the neighborhood was tense and taut, hovering on the edge of conflict and frequently slipping over the edge.

A gang rumble can start in a thousand ways. The rumble of the Cobras on Beaver Street was unusual only in that it was carried out almost at a moment's notice. Often a gang

---

* Ten months after the rumble Ricky's brother was shot to death by a policeman who surprised him with two companions beating up a Puerto Rican boy.

spends a week in reconnaissance of an enemy. The snakes observe the comings and goings of enemy boys. They find out what weapons they possess and how quickly they are available. The war counselor spies out the enemy terrain. He checks routes to enemy turf, fixes locations for ambushes, examines lines of attack and retreat. War plans are his business. He knows the combat strength of hostile gangs and the combinations which may attack his own club.

Street clubs have a loose superstructure of relations which, in theory, reaches even to distant parts of the city. There are two or three gangs which have chapters in many areas. One of the most notorious is the Chaplains. They claim ten or twenty troops, some in Brooklyn, some in Queens, some in the Bronx, some beyond the city out on Long Island. Or so they say. In theory, the Chaplains could throw all these forces as well as other affiliated gangs into combat at a single moment. Another group like this is the Sportsmen, originally established in the Bronx but now claiming chapters in the lower East Side, the middle West Side and a half-dozen other vicinities.

Fortunately for the city, the theory that all these groups might go into combat at the same time is largely a product of adolescent imagination. It is part of the fantasy in which the teen-age street boys live.

But to them it is a very real fantasy. One of the most articulate gang leaders whom I met, a slender, slim faced boy of eighteen with the gang nickname of Nero told me one night just how real this fantasy could be.

"You wouldn't think it," he said, "sitting in this room like we are and talking like we are. But just two years ago I was in an apartment over there in the project. In the middle of that room was a packing case—a big case. And in that case there were all the weapons you could imagine. There were .22 rifles, repeating rifles. There was Berettas. There was shotguns. There was everything."

Nero said his gang already was well armed. It had Mausers, a grease gun, "some kind of a machine gun" and a sawed-off shotgun.

"Oh," he said, with a grimace. "Don't worry. We had guns all right. Just like you dream about."

He and the leaders of his gang and representatives of "brother" clubs sat in the project flat and worked out a plan for an attack on the Crowns. The Crowns are a Bronx gang with several branches.

"It was crazy," Nero said. "Sure. I know that now. But we didn't think so then. It was absolutely real for us. We sat there and we got a map of the city. We figured out how many cars we could get together if we put all our brother clubs into the rumble. I don't know how many it added up to. But it was a lot. Twenty or thirty. And we figured out the routes for each of those cars. The time it would take. We calculated how many red lights they would hit and how long the different distances were from different parts of the city. We actually went out and timed those red lights."

The plan was for one great assault on the unsuspecting Crowns. Some boys would take their own cars. Others would steal them. Some would go by subway. The attack would be a complete surprise. There had been no rumble between the two groups. The theory of the operation was Hitlerian in its simplicity. The gang chiefs by wiping out one of the strongest bopping clubs would establish hegemony over all the gangs in the city. To achieve this, of course, the whole operation had to be conducted with military precision.

"One big attack," Nero said, "and it would be all over. That would be the end of the Crowns. There wouldn't be any Crowns any more. Sure, we figured on our losses, too. We knew we would lose some killed. But probably not as many as we figured. Because the Crowns wouldn't know what was coming. But we would."

The attack never came off. Such a scale of co-ordination

and planning is, fortunately, beyond the capability of the disturbed young people who make up the fighting gangs.

Arms and armament, as Nero emphasized, are not a problem for bopping gangs. Someone is always ready to sell a boy a "piece." If it happens to be "hot"—a stolen weapon or one which has been used in a holdup, the price will be only a few dollars. Five dollars for a revolver of uncertain origin is an average price. When the Little People succeed to leadership in a gang the Big People often pass on the club armory intact. If it has been lost to the police it can be replaced without much trouble. Zip guns can be made in an afternoon. This weapon was invented by some perverted adolescent genius about fifteen years ago. It utilizes rubber bands to activate a firing pin which may be a door bolt mounted on a wooden frame or the filed-down hammer of a cap pistol. It fires a .22 caliber cartridge through a barrel that is usually made of the ever-useful cylinder of the car aerial. The weapons are often made in community center hobby shops or school workrooms.

The variety of gang weapons is endless. Some possess hand grenades, dynamite-and-caps or acid bottles. One gang leader in Queens goes into battle with a can of lye into which he has urinated. Broken bottles, steel chains, lead pipes, tire irons—almost anything makes a deadly weapon in street combat.

There is a Brooklyn gang which is known to have in its arsenal half a dozen old Navy cutlasses. Machetes are common because they can be bought from a bin in many hardware stores. Some boys make Molotov cocktails (simple gasoline bombs made with a bottle and a flaming rag) such as were used by Hungarian schoolboys in the battle of Budapest.

The Beretta, a small Italian pistol brought back by many G.I.'s, is a favorite weapon in the Bronx and Manhattan. It has not yet reached Brooklyn. Most gang fighters carry knives and are proficient with them. When switchblades were outlawed they adapted easily to the gravity-blade knives put on the market by obliging manufacturers.

The automobile, where gang members have access to it, is the most feared weapon. It inspires the kind of terror among street boys that the tank aroused when it was sent against infantry in World War I. Cars are driven with lethal intent straight at enemy boys. A youngster trapped in the open street is simply run down. Survival is sheer luck.

When preparations are complete and a gang is ready to go down on another outfit the members usually rendezvous in a vacant apartment, a basement, a culvert or on a rooftop. This may be the place where the gang arsenal is cached. The fighters assemble in battle dress. A Bedford-Stuyvesant gangster wets the brim of his stenjer, rolls the rim very tight, dries it over a radiator and then pulls it down low on his head, almost over the ears. He dons a large metal medallion (made by his girl friend) and sometimes sticks his girl's ear clasp in one ear. If they have them, the boys wear their heavy leather jackets, a kind of "mail," that provides considerable protection against knife thrusts and the whiplash of car aerials. White boys wear "stomping" boots, heavy hobnails or Army shoes. They wear and use as weapons heavy webbed, brass-studded garrison belts. Many Negro fighters are too poor to afford combat boots.

At the rendezvous the boys pass around a bottle of wine. They drink and tell each other what they will do when they fall on the enemy boys. They recall past insults and injuries. The wine bottle goes around and around. Tempers rise higher and higher. By the time two or three bottles have been consumed the group roars out in a frenzy. It is ready to attack anyone who has the bad luck to fall in its path.

Not all battles are sneak attacks. There are formal staged battles, arranged by consultation between gang leaders. These may take place in a dead-end street, a wire-fenced schoolyard (at night when no one is around) or, not infrequently, a deserted corner of a park. Such a battle is usually planned as "a fair one." This means that only weapons agreed upon by the leaders are to be used. It may be a bare-knuckle fist fight. Sometimes, it is a contest of champions—the two gang leaders fighting hand to hand with fists or knives.

A "fair one" is also used by gang leaders to settle quarrels among followers. He may order two boys to have a fair one and force them to shake hands and make up when the fight is over.

However, in practice the fair one often degenerates into a catch-as-catch-can brawl. A boy pulls a forbidden knife from his pocket or draws a zip gun at a critical moment. Most fair ones wind up in a no-holds-barred riot.

To the experienced eye gang fighters en route to a rumble are easily spotted even though they move in groups of two and three in order to avoid the attention of the police. When the Cobras are going down, for example, they walk with a different stride, a kind of strut and bounce, thrusting the shoulders out and swaying their hips. This spells aggression to every street boy.

"Man," one said, "it makes you mad just to see them walk like that. You say, 'Walk straight there, man. Straighten up when you walk by me.' You can't help saying that. The moment you do the trouble is on."

What one gang regards as a *casus belli* may go unnoticed by another. Status and social attitude have much to do with determining what is considered a provocation or insult.

Gangs in Bedford-Stuyvesant, for example, live in terrible deprivation. They possess little and fear that they may lose what little they have. If a jacket is stolen they react with violence. If a stranger comes into their lounge they bristle. To these groups the concept of "our turf" is extremely important. They will fight any threat to their meager assets. These are boys who wolf down six, seven or eight hamburgers if you take them into a lunch counter. They have no idea when they may eat again. If they go on a cook-out they will steal the hotdogs, certain that there cannot possibly be enough for everyone. Food and clothing are precious to them. They will go down on a gang because of the theft of a cap.

Gangs with predominantly Puerto Rican membership present another aspect. These youngsters are new to the community. They do not know the customs, the language, the culture. They suffer deeply from affronts to their esteem. They are easily provoked by insults, real or imagined. A "sounding" sets them off. It outrages their dignity. A shove causes them to flare in anger. "You cannot imagine how insulting it is to a Puerto Rican the first time he is pushed around in the New York subway," a Puerto Rican woman said. The touch of a stranger's hand may cause a Puerto Rican boy to reach for his knife in almost a reflex action.

Italian street groups are just the opposite. They are used to fist fights. Physical contact is not offensive to them. They laugh or sneer at "sounding" but seldom think it is worth more than a retaliatory shower of verbal abuse. "Mother" swearing, which sets off both Puerto Rican and Negro lads, provokes the Italian boy to an even more imaginative demonstration of gutter phraseology. But if an alien gang invades the Italian street, if a Puerto Rican boy starts to date an Italian girl—this can quickly provoke a rumble.

Another psychology is represented by some of the Irish groups. There is one in the South Bronx, for example. They have been pushed out of several areas in which they once were kings. They see themselves as the landed aristocracy of the streets, loyal defenders of a beseiged demesne, vigilant protectors of a losing cause. They imagine their parks, their streets, their houses and their institutions being engulfed by an alien wave. This rouses them to violent aggression.

Peace between combat gangs is usually restored through conferences which have as their purpose the establishment of a "cool." When a cool is on between the Cobras and the

Rovers the Cobras permit the Rovers to walk through the area of the housing project without attack. However, if groups of more than six or seven Rovers start to cross the grounds they will be warned that such large concentrations are not friendly. The cool means that Cobras have the same freedom on the Rovers' turf.

It is not easy to establish a cool. Feelings run high. There are constant incidents. Adults as well as adolescents are upset. (Sometimes, the Rovers indulge in what Smokey calls "that father-and-mother stuff." By this he means they raid the project, attacking anyone in sight—adults, teen-agers, little children.) To an extent, I am sure, teen-age street warfare reflects hostility of adult groups. Children sometimes are overtly encouraged to attack other children. They may act out hostilities which are only verbalized by their parents.

Truces sometimes come about because both sides grow weary of combat. Street fighting is no fun, as the boys repeatedly told me. It is a grim, dangerous, frightening business. No boy knows whether he is going to get through the day alive or whether his knife may kill another boy before nightfall.

The question of loss of face and of rep complicates the establishment of a cool. Sometimes, an accident will lead to a truce. This happened once with Smokey after a long combat between the Cobras and Apaches. Life in the community had been torn to ribbons for weeks. Smokey was working days and jitterbugging at night. One evening he took a short cut home from work across Apache territory. They captured him. The Apaches could have killed Smokey. They could have tortured him. Such things happen to street boys. But the Apaches were tired of fighting. They took Smokey to their hangout, produced a bottle of wine and proposed a cool. They would free him without harm if he would call off the war. Smokey had no real alternative. Besides, he was equally tired of the fight. He agreed to the terms and the cool was on.

One of the difficult problems handled by the street workers of the New York City Youth Board is the arranging of cools. This requires as much finesse as a summit conference. It may take two weeks of stubborn talk to persuade a gang to have "a meet" with its enemy. The session is held on neutral ground. Usually some important neighborhood figure is brought in as impartial chairman to give status to the occasion.

The scene is set with care. Ashtrays, paperweights, clipboards, ink bottles, letter openers, movable files, wastebaskets —any possible weapon is cleared from the room. Three or four muscular playground instructors are brought in as advisors. They hover watchfully in the background. The gang plenipotentiaries are frisked before entering the conference room. Once, when this precaution was omitted, a boy whipped out a switchblade in the middle of an argument. The impartial chairman dove under the table and the "meet" came to an inglorious end. The rival groups arrive at different times to avoid the possibility of fatal collisions.

Andrei Gromyko never haggled as much as do the gang diplomats. They have an endless catalog of grievances which must be "set straight" before a cool can be arranged. "Let's get this straight, man," a leader says.

Every insult, every rumor of an insult, every ambush, every knife wound is enumerated, one by one. For each item on the enemy list the other gang has a twin. Gradually, the grievances are talked out and finally a few underlying points of substance may emerge. There may, perhaps, be a cloudy question of turf—the matter of access to a particular spot in the other's area—the home of a girl, the apartment of a boy's aunt. This may be regulated like a United Nations team settling the issue of access to the shrines of Jerusalem. Visits will be permitted but only at certain hours and by small groups. There may be a question of property loss—a jacket bearing the club insignia has been stolen, the jukebox in the club lounge has been vandalized. Perhaps it is agreed to return the jacket. The claim of damage to the jukebox is matched against the broken windows in the enemy's community center. An unprovoked insult to a girl may finally be admitted and an apology offered. Some effort is directed toward minimizing future conflict—promises to consult between leaders before any attack. When all the chaff has been sifted it may be clear that the rumble was started because of a false rumor or a misapprehension. It turns out that Vice was not japped by the Apaches as the Cobras had thought. It was, instead, a group of Viceroys from uptown who happened to be passing through the neighborhood. Or the tale which Vickey told about being grabbed by two of the Cobras and having her dress torn may prove to have been just another of Vickey's stories. The cost of Vickey's maneuver is never added up. But it can easily run as high as several boys sent to the hospital, many more put into jail, property destroyed and thousands of dollars' expenditure of time and trouble by police and social workers.

All of this because Vickey tore her dress, scuffling with another girl, and invented the story, partly to get attention and partly, no doubt, to avoid a bawling-out from her mother.

After all the sweat and toil of establishing a cool it may be ephemeral. The very next night some shook-up youngster may jab his knife into another's side, starting the whole dreary process into motion again.

"These are not rational adults," a worker emphasized. "Sometimes, they talk with great charm and logic. But these are upset, immature youngsters. One moment they are cool and reasonable. The next moment they are running up the street like a pack of wolves in full pursuit of another frightened youngster."

The institution of the rumble has reached its most complex development in New York. Rumbles occur throughout the metropolitan area. They have been increasingly common

since the end of World War II. They are familiar in cities
like Newark, Jersey City and Yonkers (although they may be
blamed on kids from New York). They happen in Trenton
and Camden and Philadelphia. Somewhat less convention-
alized gang fighting is frequent in other big cities—Chicago,
Cleveland, Pittsburgh and Baltimore. But in the open cities
of the West, the Midwest and the Southwest where almost
every teen-ager has access to an automobile there is a behavior
pattern which clearly can be attributed to environmental
differences.

The small-town cousins of the Cobras do not bop with
the local Apaches. They utilize their cars as engines of mutual
destruction. The shook-up kids of the Midwest attack a hostile adolescent group in their souped-up cars. They overrun
the enemy cars on the highway and force them off the shoulder. A fatal accident often results. Sometimes, two or three
cars roar down on an ordinary citizen who is peacefully driving along the freeway. The youngsters make successive passes
at their victim until they crowd him off the highway. State
highway police believe that not a few crashes involving cars
which mysteriously run off open highways can be attributed
to youthful car gangsters.

These same kids raid the highway diner whose proprietor
has kicked them out for drinking. They come back after he
has closed up and wreck the joint. These are the youngsters
who hold up highway filling stations "for kicks." Their
nervous fingers often press the trigger and shoot down a victim almost by accident.

Their conflict with society differs from that of the Cobras
very little. But because their life is dominated by the automobile and the highway these become the instruments of
their rebellion.

Sometimes the street conflict of the New York gangs is
romanticized. *West Side Story* has made it the subject of a
touching, tragic musical with a Romeo and Juliet theme.

Desperate as is the tragedy of *West Side Story* it fails to catch the black despair of the rumble and the impermanent cool.

Not often does street conflict, even if a victory is scored, lead a gang into anything but more trouble. It is just one stage in an ever-descending progress toward a final debacle of violence.

But once in a great while the tables are turned and the gang in the street wins a clear-cut victory. Some years ago this happened up in Harlem. Near 125th Street there was an active bopping gang which went under the name of the Young Turks. The Turks were turbulent youngsters, constantly fighting a neighboring gang called the Dark Angels.

There was a vacant building in the block where the Turks had their hangout. One afternoon a moving van pulled up, unloaded filing cases, desks, office equipment under the watchful eyes of several tan-suited, shoulder-padded, hip-bulging, sharp-eyed men. A couple of days later one of the tan-suited men sought out Sonny, the leader of the Turks.

"Get your kids off this block," the sharp-eyed man said. "We don' want no trouble around here. No cops, no fights. Cool it—get what I mean?"

"Who you talking for?" Sonny asked.

"No damn questions," the sharp-eyed man said. "You damn well know who runs things around here. Now get scarce. And remember. We don' want no cops messin' round this block. And we don' want no reason for no cops messin' round."

Sonny reported his conversation to his pals.

"Thinks he's a big shot," Sonny said. "Just because he's a Syndicate man. Thinks he can come on our turf and order us around. Wise guy."

Street warfare went on. The Turks and the Angels paid no attention to the warning. A night or two later the block was choked with squad cars, summoned to halt a rumble. The Syndicate got mad. It had a big investment to protect and it didn't want street kids jeopardizing that investment. The next night when the kids congregated on the street a couple of the sharp-eyed, tan-suited young men sauntered out, drew their pistols and fired a fusillade or two over the heads of the kids. The kids ran—but not far.

The following night they threw rocks through the windows of the Syndicate building. The night after they did the same thing.

A week later a Youth Board supervisor had a strange visitor. He was an indignant representative of the Syndicate.

"Look, man," the Syndicate representative said, "you gotta do something about those kids in the block off 125th Street. They got no sense, these kids. They smash up the street every night. Cops come down there two, three times an evening. How long you think we can operate in a place like that? We're businessmen. We don't want no trouble. You gotta get those kids off our back. They're crazy. They don't care what they do."

The Youth Board worker conveyed the Syndicate message to Sonny.

"Tell 'em to shove it," Sonny said. "What's a-matter with those guys? We're just kids. What they mean shooting at us? Ain't no big people going to shoot at us and get away with it. We weren't doing them no harm. That's our turf. It don't belong to no Syndicate or nobody but us. They got no right to move in on us. We're just kids. They don't like it—they can punk out."

Which is what the Syndicate did. Despairing of ever calling it cool with their adolescent antagonists the Syndicate ordered in the moving van—and punked out.

4

the shook-up kids

I MET Smokey on the first night that I spent in Schroeder's candy store. It was cold on the Brooklyn streets that February evening. The temperature stood at eighteen or twenty and the wind was brisk. It seemed to me that Brooklyn, or at least the places the kids hung out, was always colder than anywhere else. In such weather the corner is no fun. The few youngsters who turned out came inside the candy store. They played the juke, riffled through the rack of comic books and peered, from time to time, through the frosted window into the street.

As the boys straggled into the candy store a street club worker introduced me to them. I was impressed by the limp handshake each gave me and I asked the worker about it. He laughed.

"They don't know you," he said. "They aren't sure whether you are a friend or enemy. They shake hands—but not very strongly because they don't know how far to trust you."

After three or four meetings I noticed that the handclasps were growing firmer. I had won a measure of their uncertain confidence.

Smokey was a little different from the start. Possibly, being a leader, he had more self-confidence. At any rate his grip was almost normal. We exchanged only a few words that evening. I noticed that he was dressed better than most of his companions. He wore a warm tan toggle coat and black beret on which he had pinned a tufted ornament. The radiators in the candy store didn't give much heat so he kept his coat on all evening. His smile was easy but I could see it wash off his face when he stepped into a corner to confer with his lieutenants. The other boys deferred to Smokey. Several times he flipped a hand at a boy. The youngster stepped up quickly, Smokey whispered a word or two in his ear and the boy hurried off, obviously carrying an order to someone or delivering a message.

Many gang members are deficient in intelligence. They may never have ventured beyond a few blocks from their homes. Sometimes, they are so illiterate that they cannot ride the subway because they cannot read the names of the stations. I have met boys who could not articulate their words and had difficulty in using speech. They did not seem to be able to fit words to ideas. I was puzzled to know how they communicated with each other.

Smokey, on the other hand, was a boy whom you would notice in any group. I liked him from my first meeting. He had an air of assurance and authority that was unmistakable. He talked easily and his mind was quick. Not that he did well in school. Several weeks later I had a long discussion with him.

"I do all right in school," he said. "Of course, I could do much better if I put my mind to it. All I do is pass. I could be an honor student. That's no crap. But you know how it is. The boys are always suggesting—you do this, you do that. So you don't have the courage of your convictions. You are per-suaded."

Smokey laughed wryly.

"I was per-suaded today," he said. "Some of the Chaplains

had a bottle in school. If I'm a little fuzzy it's because we were drinking all day."

The Chaplains and the Cobras are enemies, but the boys do not usually carry their quarrels to school.

"I couldn't refuse to drink with them," he explained. "I couldn't punk out. I had to show them that the Cobras could drink better than the Chaplains."

When Smokey got to talking he had few inhibitions and he discussed himself and his problems with considerable insight. I found that street youngsters reacted to serious questions with serious answers. When they are convinced that you are sincere they reveal a pathetic eagerness to talk about themselves. It is not often that they encounter an adult who really cares what their life is like. Probably 95 per cent of them come from broken families or families in name only. They get neither understanding nor interest at home. Home life is apt to be a compound of neglect, curses, beatings and drink. This did not hold true for Smokey, nor many other gang leaders. These boys are superior to their comrades and their homes are usually superior. Smokey had a good family, a warm family. His father and mother had been strict in bringing him up, possibly too strict. But they were concerned about his welfare and they loved him. In his way Smokey was concerned about them, too. He loved his mother and regarded his father with a mixture of respect and affection.

Smokey said he was seventeen. He was born in Florida but he was brought north when he was so small that he did not remember it. He had a younger brother and three younger sisters. The other children were doing well in school. If Smokey could help it his brother would not get mixed up in the gang. He himself never jitterbugged until he was thirteen or fourteen. Then he was drafted by the Cobra Juniors.

"I wish I could of stayed out," he says now. "But there is no real alternative. If you stay out they beat you up. Maybe

you complain to a policeman. What is he going to do about
it? Maybe he gets the guys who did it. But what about the
next time? He can't keep it from happening again. So you
might as well join."

Smokey was seriously worried about his future. He insisted
that he hated and feared street fighting.

"People don't understand," he said. "I would much rather
not bop. Nobody wants to bop. It isn't any fun to bop. If you
are going down on somebody your heart is going to beat
faster. You don't know what will happen. You may be killed.
Or you may kill someone. Nobody knows. If anyone goes
down and isn't afraid it just means he don't know what he's
doing."

At seventeen Smokey was thinking a great deal about the
gang and what it implied. He was thinking about getting out.

"I'll be through with school in June," he said. "I figure
on going in the Army. I know it's about time for me to be
giving up the gang. So far I've been very lucky. Very lucky.
So far I've never been hurt. And I've never hurt anyone." (In
street language "hurt" means to kill or seriously wound.)
"But this can't go on forever. I don't want to get arrested.
I don't want to get involved in killing someone. But if this
goes on someone will get killed. On one side or another. You
never know. It can be you."

Smokey had definite ambitions. The ordinary gang member
does not. He often has no perspective beyond the street. He
counts it an achievement just to get through today or this
week or this month. He can see no further.

"Would you think it funny if I said that my real ambition
was to become a policeman?" Smokey asked. "I don't know
whether I can be now. But I know that I want to stay out of
jail and I want to get out of this."

Smokey discussed his mother and father with deep feeling.
It would be terrible if he caused them trouble. They thought
so much of him. His father was a machinist. He had a good

job. His parents did not know he was in a bopping club. They suspected. But they weren't sure.

"There isn't anything that would hurt me more," Smokey said, "than to cause them worry or trouble, to be arrested or to get into some kind of trouble like that. That's where there's a conflict. Between what you should do and what you want to do."

When he spoke of his gang Smokey revealed the nature of this conflict clearly.

"I love every one of them!" he said of the gang. "Well, I mean I like them. I would do anything for those boys. A leader has to have a sense of responsibility for his men. Like right now. There's all kinds of police in the district. I give my men orders. Not to walk around more than two or three together. It's too dangerous. Don't start anything. The cops are just waiting to pick you up."

I wondered how Smokey was going to resolve the conflict between his feelings for his family and for his gang. Perhaps it was beyond his powers to resolve. Perhaps life would have to resolve it for him.

Smokey had a job as a messenger boy with a firm in Manhattan. He was going "almost steady" with a girl who had moved out of the neighborhood.

Looking to the future he said: "After I am through the service—if I get in the service—maybe I'll get married. Maybe I'll have to get married. But then I don't want to come back here. By that time the Little People will be running the club. I want to be far away and out of it. Because if I come back here I'll still be in it. The bopping will still be going on. It won't change. And it's that way all over the city."

Again and again I encountered among the gangs this conviction of the inevitability of conflict on the streets. To these youngsters it seemed a pattern of existence that would go on forever.

It was early March when I had that conversation with

Smokey. Six weeks passed before I heard anything more about him. What I heard was not pleasant. A lot had happened in those six weeks. But nothing good.

A few days after our talk Smokey had been arrested on a charge of assault and extortion. He had beaten up a boy and taken money from him. This was serious. It was made more serious by the fact that Smokey was already on probation. The jerry-built structure of Smokey's life started to collapse immediately. The truth about his gang activity could no longer be concealed from his parents. His father had to get a lawyer to defend Smokey and obtain his release on bail. This put his father into debt by $300. Even so, the chances were good that the court would send Smokey up for a term in reformatory.

When the housing project manager heard of Smokey's arrest he gave the family an eviction notice. At the end of two months they must move. Where they would find a new place they had no idea. But certainly it would cost $200 or $300 key money—another trip to the loan shark.

Because he was in jail for a week Smokey lost his job.

Because it no longer seemed to make any difference Smokey quit school.

His girl, only fifteen, discovered that she was pregnant. Smokey said he didn't care. He stopped going with her and started running around with other girls.

This is all that has happened to Smokey so far. It is a good bet that other bad things are coming. He is drinking more now. Without school, without work, without his girl, with his parents disturbed and angry, with the threat of prison hanging over him, Smokey is retreating from the world. Drink and the gang provide a temporary escape. But his leadership of the gang is not as assured as it was a few months ago. He is belligerent, ready to fight anyone. The gang is getting into more and more trouble.

Only a miracle can save Smokey now. But in the world

of the street boy miracles are even more rare than they are in our world. What has happened to Smokey is more than a bitter personal tragedy. It is symbolic of the fate which awaits most of Smokey's comrades. Smokey is exceptional only because he has more intelligence, more ability. He has, however, a fatal weakness—the need and desire for the adulation of his fellows. In another environment this might have spurred him to classroom success or athletic triumph. But in Smokey's neighborhood there is only one place where a boy can star. That is the street.

The street is the only life which Seven Up knows. He is an undersized youngster of sixteen with scars on his forehead and on the back of his closely clipped head—battle wounds. He was brought to New York seven years ago from a South Carolina farm. His parents died soon thereafter. Seven Up has been passed from hand to hand ever since. One distant relative after another. No one wanted him. Now he lives with an elderly aunt who is on relief. The old lady is barely able to move about. She makes no attempt to care for Seven Up.

Seven Up is a member of the Cobras. He wears a dirty gray jacket that needs mending. He has a quick smile and a twisted sense of humor. His poverty is complete. He is often hungry. There are days when he goes all day without food. He can read simple words in big type. He can write his name. Otherwise he is illiterate.

There is no one to whom Seven Up has the slightest importance except the Cobras. The school is happier when he does not show up. His aunt is past any interest in him. No one cares what happens to Seven Up. He often injects the phrase "if I live" or "if I don't die" into his conversation. It seems natural. Like many desperately poor, desperately deprived youngsters he is famous for one thing—"heart." This brings affection and acclaim from his gang. They are his world and if he can win their warmth by defying the adult world, well, the price is cheap to Seven Up. Anyone in his situation, I suspect, would feel the same. It is hard to think what society has done for Seven Up which would warrant his feeling toward it any respect, duty or obligation.

Chocolate might be Seven Up's brother, his situation is so similar. He belongs to a Bedford-Stuyvesant gang. He is sixteen, a short youngster with a faraway gleam in his eye. He has been in state institutions several times. He came out recently and certainly will return soon—if he is not killed first. This boy is more illiterate than Seven Up. In the words of a friend "he couldn't read 'New York' if the letters were as big as a truck." He is drunk from early morning until late at night. He probably uses narcotics. His mental condition is dubious. But he has heart to a suicidal degree. Chocolate is past the point where he can really recognize danger, if, indeed, he ever had any clear conception of the risks he has taken. He is, in the understatement of a social worker "a very sick boy." Nothing good will ever happen to Chocolate. There is really no reason why he should not court death. It could not possibly be more unkind to him than life has been.

Pepito isn't as shook-up as Chocolate. Not yet. But he is only fourteen. At his present pace he will be lucky to reach sixteen. When I saw Pepito in the playroom of the community center I did not guess that he smoked marijuana. Nor would I have thought that he sniffed heroin occasionally. His hair is plastered over his forehead in a Sal Mineo cowlick and his face has a babyish quality. His eyes are brown and sulky and he looks like a spoiled younger brother as he plays table tennis—quick, active, alert and a little edgy. I did not pick him as one of the most shook-up members of the Silver Arrows. But the boys agreed that he was. He was on probation for shoplifting and narrowly had escaped being picked up for purse snatching. Almost every evening he walked into the community house, munching a slab of pastry he had swiped off a bakery truck. No one in the neighborhood would turn in Pepito for such petty thievery. They knew how often he went without meals.

When I met Pepito he was living with a grandmother on relief. She could not manage him. He seldom bothered to go to school. Even within the gang he was quarrelsome and irresponsible. But the gang valued him. He had heart. He would do things no other boy would dare. He would sound a cop on the beat and run away laughing. In a rumble he was like a wildcat.

Pepito knew nothing of the world beyond his neighborhood. He "read" the pictures in comic books and was enchanted with the gunplay of cowboy movies.

Soon after I met Pepito he was taken by his father to live up in the Bronx. I thought this might get the boy off to a fresh start. For a short time it seemed that it had. Pepito came back to his old hangout, saying the life in the Bronx was terrible, the kids were no good, there was nothing to do. But a few weeks later he turned up tougher and more self-confident than ever. Two friends, leather-jacket lads like himself, came with him. He told his old gang that things were not so bad in the Bronx after all. "Come up and see our club sometimes," he said. "We got some good bops."

Pepito's life in the Bronx had gotten back on the same tracks it followed in Brooklyn. The progression is hard to change.

There is nothing to distinguish the Chimp from any other overgrown eighteen-year-old high school boy. He sits in the candy store with a Coke in front of him. There are five boys in all, crowded into a booth built for four. All are drinking Cokes. Across from them are four girls, drinking sodas. It is the kind of scene you can see in any town of America, any day of the week around nine of an evening. It would make a good cover for the *Saturday Evening Post*. The girls have pony-tail hairdos which they keep inspecting in the wall mirror. Most of the boys have butch haircuts. The boys are talking among themselves but they keep eying the girls. Several boys and several girls wear white-and-maroon school sweaters.

These boys are Rovers. Most Rovers are Italian or Irish although there is one Negro member and two Puerto Ricans. The Chimp is one of the leadership clique even though his status is not too high. The Chimp, unfortunately, has a tendency to "punk out" when the fighting gets tough. His uncle was a famous Brooklyn gangster whose name made many headlines. His father, his uncles, his brothers all work on the docks.

The Chimp is a good deal brighter than most of his companions. He is more intelligent than his record indicates. He was expelled from parochial school. He did no better in public high school. He skipped the last year by getting a fake doctor's certificate of ill health. He worked instead.

But the Chimp understands more about himself than most gang youngsters. He realizes that bravery is not his long suit. When I met him he was about to be inducted into the Army. Army induction in this neighborhood is an occasion—presents from parents, going-away parties and a grand all-night liquor party the evening before reporting.

The Chimp was looking forward to getting into the Army. "I hope the Army will make a man of me," he said. He meant he hoped it would cure his lack of nerve. Also he hoped it would lead him away from the docks. He did not want to follow in the footsteps of his father and uncles. His chief interests were quite different—jazz, dancing (he has won several competitions) and hi-fi. Like most of his group he likes *Confidential* magazine. Reading about the scandalous conduct of persons who are well known or important makes the Chimp feel that he has done nothing very bad. "So what have I ever done?" he says. "Geez, I never stole anything big. These people—they get away with murder and I do mean murder."

He watches the horror movies on the television late late shows and tries to catch Dick Clark's late-afternoon TV rock 'n' roll show from Philadelphia. A New York radio station with a disc jockey who caters to candy-store cliques is a favorite of his. He and other adolescents telephone in messages all evening long. "Greetings from the gang in the Kandy Kitchen of Delmar Avenue," "Al of 159th Street, the Bronx, sends his regards to the boys and girls at Joe's Candy Store," "Christine wishes a big hello to the bunch on the Bronx Concourse." On at least one occasion these broadcasts have been used for inter-gang communication—to set up arrangements for a rumble.

The Chimp and his friends spend more time looking at television than do the Cobras or Arrows. Last summer they watched a TV play which told how the Communists had gained control of a corporation and used their power to wreck the company and throw a lot of people out of jobs. When the Chimp's good friend, Steve, lost his job in the merger of a steel firm he knew the answer.

"The Commies must of got ahold of that company," Steve says. "It's happening every day now. Lookit all the unemployed there are."

Steve doesn't mind unemployment. He gets his benefits. He describes himself now as "a free air inspector." He says he is too busy to work. There is some truth in that. If he got a job he would not have so much time to spend at the candy store.

The Chimp makes no secret of the fact that he hopes to leave the neighborhood someday. A psychologist might say that the Chimp is revolting against his family and the whole waterfront environment of violence and brutality. This may be so. But few youngsters in this area escape. The normal evolution is from participation in the teen-age Rovers to participation in adult gangs on the docks—from little crime and juvenile violence to big crime and adult violence.

"Sometimes, guys come to work on the docks," the Chimp

says sagely. "They hope to make money, save it and get away and go into business. But they never make it. How can they? Where else can you earn that kind of dough?"

This is a bitter lesson which the Chimp himself probably will learn. His hopes for utilizing the Army as a bridge out of his environment overlooked one important fact. The Chimp had a police record. After all the parties, all the presents, all the drinking the Chimp came back to the block less than a month later. He only lasted in the Army long enough for the electronic computors to turn up his larceny conviction.

I think that only one among the young people in the candy store that night had a reasonable chance of breaking the pattern. This was Maureen, a tall mature brunette of eighteen. She talked very frankly and looked you in the eye as she talked. She was in her last year of parochial high school. She wanted to go to college. "But not with the sisters, thank you," she laughed. "I've had twelve years with them. They are very nice and all that but enough is enough. I'm going upstate. To a teachers' college."

The girl sitting next to Maureen was called Flora. She was a blonde with wide blue eyes and heavily painted lips. She didn't pay any attention to Maureen's talk. There was a bridge of freckles over her nose and traces of a tan. Flora had only been back home two weeks from Florida. She went there with a married man who kept her a month and then put her on a bus for home. No one thought the worse of Flora for this. She had come right back to the candy store. If a boy wanted to take her out in his car that was fine. If another boy wanted her when they got back that was okay, too. She was just sitting around, waiting for something to turn up. Maybe another man who would like to take her to Florida. Or possibly California. It didn't really make any difference.

Maureen did not disapprove of Flora. If Flora wanted to go with men that was Flora's business. It just wasn't Maureen's style, that was all. Nor was Maureen like Annabella, the dark-haired Italian girl with ruby cheeks who sat across from her. Annabella had a single-track mind. She wanted a boy to go steady with, a boy who had a job and who wanted to get married. Annabella wanted to get married. Nothing else made the slightest difference. When she went out with boys she didn't let them fool around. Not unless they wanted to get married. Some girls said she was foolish. That wasn't the way to get a boy. Let him make love. Get pregnant. When the baby was coming he would have to marry you. Maybe the girls were right. So far Annabella wasn't sure. If she didn't get a boy this year maybe she would change her tactics. She would see.

Maureen laughed at Annabella.

"Go steady if you want to," she said. "Go ahead and get married. Have your babies. As for me, I'm not going steady. There's not a boy in the world I would go steady with. First, I'm going to college. Maybe I'll meet somebody there. One thing I'll tell you, I'm going to get out of this dump. And never come back."

It will take a year or two to test Maureen's determination. But she had a better chance of success than the boys. Her parents were backing her. Her father earned enough money on the docks to send her to school. He was not a heavy drinker. Maureen was a strong, tough girl. If a boy used filthy language, and the boys liked to use obscenity before girls, Maureen told him off in the same words. She knew them all. If a boy got rough with her she knew where to hit him so it would hurt most.

I did not meet many youngsters of Maureen's tenacity but I did not meet a single gang leader who did not say that he wanted to break out of the pattern of street life. I think the boys are sincere in this. The difficulty lies in their ignorance of how to go about it and their lack of strength to cope with stubborn reality.

This seemed to be the case with Tommy, the leader of one branch of the Chaplains. Tommy told me that he was almost seventeen but I would have guessed his age at fourteen. He is a thin, birdlike youngster with a muscle on the side of his face that twitches nervously. He does not dress like a bop. He wears a neat felt hat, tan windbreaker, red sweater, neat dark tie, white shirt, ordinary black shoes. He was busy collecting money from his members when I met him.

"We're going to buy some sweaters," he said. "They'll have 'C' on them—'C' for Casanova not Chaplains. Do you think the police will believe it when we say 'C' is for Casanova?"

I doubted very much if the police or anyone else would believe such a story.

Tommy was born in Georgia and has been back there for summer vacations. He didn't like it because the "people are too old-fashioned." By this he meant that he was made to go to bed at ten o'clock.

Tommy does not get along well with his parents. His mother, father and brother work. There is no lack of money in the home. They live in public housing. The family is gone all day and Tommy is supposed to take care of the house. He gets an allowance of $1.75 a week. This is far more than any of his gang comrades receives. But he is not satisfied.

"That's just enough for bubble gum," he says, in contempt. He would rather skip the allowance if he could get out of housework. He receives passing grades but doesn't like school. His favorite subject, he says with a sneer, is "lunch."

"What do you like to read?" I asked him.

"Nothin'," he replied. "I don't like to read."

"What do you like to do?"

"Sit."

"Just sit?"

"Just sit."

He was sardonic about his ambitions. "What do I want to do in life?" he asked. "Stay alive. Some people say I won't live so long."

This was not just adolescent bravado. Tommy had nine stitches taken in his scalp after an encounter with the Bishops on New Year's Eve. "I was drunk," he said. "I got careless. But we made it up to them."

Tommy likes very few things in his life. He dislikes his home, his school, the neighborhood (he would like to live in a house in the country) and the gang. He does not like sports. Football is too rough. He doesn't follow baseball. He couldn't think of any heroes, neither prize fighters nor soldiers. Like all gang kids he is ready to risk his life in combat with knife or gun but he won't go out to fight in the rain. He doesn't want to spoil his clothes. He has never owned a cat or dog. He would like to work in an office where "it is clean and you can dress nice." He is another boy who looks to the Army as a possible escape from the vicious circle of his life. When I asked if he'd rather there were no gangs he said: "Oh, yes! Then, we'd be able to go everywhere freely and keep all strangers off our turf."

Why didn't he like strangers?

"Because," he said, with a small boy's petulance, "one night one would come down. The next night there would be two. And the next night three and pretty soon they'd be all over the place."

Perhaps the most impressive gang leader whom I met was Vincent, the slender Puerto Rican leader of the Silver Arrows. Vincent is seventeen. He looks a little like an Aztec prince, his black hair combed in a massive crest and his head carried high. When Vincent came from Puerto Rico in 1949 his family first settled in Manhattan on the edge of East Harlem. He likes Brooklyn much better for a reason which any street boy would understand.

"I hate Manhattan," Vincent said, shuddering. "Those

square blocks! You walk into a block—they can jap you
anywhere. There is no way out of them. Once you are in
a block you have to go to the end. You can't escape. It is
terrible."

Vincent thinks Brooklyn is wonderful:

"All those curved streets, going this way and that way.
You can always run somewhere. You can get away."

Security, security, security. This is close to the surface of
almost everything the youngsters do or say. Want of security
is what leads them into the gang and want of security is what
keeps them in this dangerous limbo.

Vincent was introduced to street fighting by the Italian
boys in the neighborhood into which his family first moved.
They beat him up many times. Finally, he joined their gang.
When he came to Brooklyn his street experience enabled
him to take leadership of the Puerto Rican boys in Whitman
Houses.

It had been Vincent's hope that he might become an
aviation mechanic. He was enrolled in Aviation High School
and did fair work there. But he quit school the day before
his graduation when he learned that because he had a police
record he could not get a certificate. Vincent is bitter over
this. He was charged with stealing a pistol from a National
Guard Armory and he says the charge was false.

"That's the way it starts," he said. "I've seen it happen
many times. The police blame you for something you didn't
do. You get a record. They send you away. So, then, the
kid comes back and he says, 'Well, I'm going to do something and get a record of my own. At least then if I'm sent
up it will be for something I did myself.' "

When that happens, Vincent says, there is no holding
a youngster. He will go on and on and on until finally he
is caught and sent back to prison. I think he is right about
this. Even among the small sampling of youngsters whom

I got to know it seemed to me that the number who were falsely accused by the police was about as great as those who were justly accused. This was a source of great bitterness. One reason for this, of course, is that boys do not come forward and admit their guilt even when a friend is held for the crime which they committed.

There is also a certain resignation to fate. Vincent, for example, was given an opportunity for legal assistance in reopening the question of his high school certificate. But he never bothered to get in touch with the lawyer. He didn't really believe it would be of any use.

Vincent comes from a big poor family. He lives with his mother and father and eight brothers and sisters. The family has been on relief for several years. Vincent is the only one who is involved with gangs.

"I'm the only bad one," he says, almost shame-faced. "My mother knows that I fight. She asks me what I am doing and I tell her. I tell her I only fight when I have to. For some good reason. She does not like this but she understands this. I do not like it either. But what is there to do? That is the way it is."

Now that his chance of getting a job as an aviation mechanic has vanished Vincent doesn't know what to do. He worked for a while in a machine shop but he had to get up so early and travel so far that he quit.

"I don't know," he said. "I don't know what there is for me to do. The only thing I want to do I can't do. So it doesn't make much difference."

Vincent says that he bears no grudges against the boys with whom he fights "except for a few." He says he would like a permanent cool but "they won't have it that way." He doesn't think the police can stop the fighting.

"The trouble with the police is the way they look at you," he says. "We are standing on the corner. The cop comes along. He tells you to move along. If he treated you like you were people—but he doesn't. He has that hard look. I just can't stand to have cops look at me like that."

Vincent, like his comrades, feels that there will be no end to street fighting.

"The only way to stop it would be for you to be free to go anywhere in the city and nobody would touch you," he said. "Then there would be no fighting. But somebody will always interfere. One fellow will start it and then it is on again. That's the way it is."

Vincent had come uptown to have dinner in a restaurant with me where we could talk with a freedom that was not possible in the candy store or community house. We finished our coffee and went out into the brisk air of an early March evening. I walked a little way with Vincent and stood with him while he waited for his bus. The sky was clear and the stars were sparkling dust against the dark space of the universe. We stood a moment and then Vincent boarded his bus, back to the housing project and the Arrows, back to his turf and his narrow island of security. I turned and headed for the subway back to Manhattan. No policeman gave me any hard looks and I was free to go anywhere I wanted to in the city. I wondered whether it was really beyond the ability of a rich city like New York to make the streets as safe and free for boys like Vincent as they were for me.

5

the new ghettos

MANY Americans have a comfortable feeling that city slums are a thing of the past. Slums are something we associate with the Triangle Shirtwaist fire, the "melting pot," the crowded and colorful life of the lower East Side at the turn of the century.

Most New Yorkers share that feeling. The city's slums, they believe, were eliminated in the days of the New Deal and Mayor La Guardia. They speed down East River Drive and marvel at the phalanxes of new structures. They congratulate themselves upon the elimination of the squalor against which Jacob Riis crusaded so long ago.

New brick towers rise along the right-of-way of the New York Central and the New Haven as the commuting trains sweep down from Connecticut and Westchester. The men from Wall Street sometimes talk about it as they fold away the *Times* and the *Tribune* and prepare to get off at Grand Central. It is remarkable, they say, the progress which is being made in the city. You can hardly recognize Harlem. The East Side has been transformed.

Driving out the Gowanus Super-Highway they admire the rectangular patterns of Fort Greene Houses, Gowanus Houses, Red Hook Houses, Queensbridge Houses. It makes you feel good, they say, to live in a country where progress happens almost overnight. Of course, they do not agree with some of the things that are being done in Washington but you have to admit that people are better taken care of than in the old days. Maybe they are treated too well. It just encourages more of them to come up from Puerto Rico and the Deep South.

This is how the people talk. I know because this is the way I talked until recently. I have been away from the United States a good deal since the war. When I came back to New York and drove the expressway around the island I hardly recognized parts of the city. The great experiment in public housing launched during the Roosevelt administration seemed to have paid off. I was amazed at the changes. Whole areas of the city had given way to fine new construction. I wished that I could take a delegation of Russians around and show them what a magnificent job we were doing in the field of public housing.

Then, last winter I visited Fort Greene Houses, Brooklyn. I was warned that most visitors preferred to walk up three or four flights instead of taking the elevator. I quickly understood why they chose the steep, cold staircases rather than face the stench of stale urine that pervades the elevators.

Until my nostrils ferreted out the fetid story of Fort Greene and until I had seen the inside of Marcy Houses and St. Nicholas Houses I was not aware that in too many instances we have merely institutionalized our slums. We have immured old horror and new deprivation behind these cold walls.

I saw shoddy housing in Moscow. Many Soviet apartment houses are built so cheaply and maintained so badly that you cannot guess from looking whether they are two years old or twenty. I have seen Moscow elevators that don't work and Moscow plumbing that stinks. But until I visited Fort Greene I had never seen elevators used by children as public toilets.

I never imagined that I could find the equivalent of Moscow's newly built slums in the United States. But I have made that unfortunate discovery at Fort Greene and other places. The same shoddy shiftlessness, the broken windows, the missing light bulbs, the plaster cracking from the walls, the pilfered hardware, the cold, drafty corridors, the doors on sagging hinges, the acid smell of sweat and cabbage, the ragged children, the plaintive women, the playgrounds that are seas of muddy clay, the bruised and battered trees, the ragged clumps of grass, the planned absence of art, beauty or taste, the gigantic masses of brick, of concrete, of asphalt, the inhuman genius with which our know-how has been perverted to create human cesspools worse than those of yesterday.

If these words seem strong, visit these massive barracks for the destitute yourself. Visit Fort Greene with its thirty-four hundred families—possibly seventeen thousand people. It is described as the world's largest housing project. It is better described as a $20,000,000 slum.

Fort Greene and projects like it are forcing centers of juvenile delinquency. They spawn teen-age gangs. They incubate crime. They are fiendishly contrived institutions for the debasing of family and community life to the lowest common mean. They are worse than anything George Orwell ever conceived.

These are strong words also. But go talk to the despairing people immured in Fort Greene. See for yourself if the words are exaggerated.

This situation would be bad if it were unavoidable and irremediable. It is neither. It was created by the perversion, part accidental, part deliberate, of a well-intended effort to eliminate a sordid social evil, the old slum. Many of these conditions are caused by blind enforcement of bureaucratic rules. Others stem from inadequate concepts, bad administration and, often, deliberate sabotage by cruel, stupid and heartless men. Some projects seem more like Golgothas designed to twist, torture and destroy the hapless people condemned to their dismal precincts than new homes for misfortunates. None of this is necessary. All of it could have been avoided.

There is a pleasant view from the window of Mrs. Angus's apartment at Fort Greene. It looks out on the one island which has been carved into the uniform rectangles of the project. On this island stands St. Edward's Church, a gray stone structure, neo-Byzantine in concept, possessing both character and strength. It is a quiet view, a relief from the planned stereotypy of the Fort Greene scheme.

"The things I have seen from this window!" Mrs. Angus sighs as she pulls aside the ragged lace curtain to look out. "You'd never guess. Terrible things."

Terrible, indeed. On a Christmas Eve two years ago a group of Italian sailors were walking through Fort Greene. They had been celebrating at a bar. How they came to enter Fort Greene is not important. Perhaps they noticed the church and thought to attend the Mass of Christmas Eve. Perhaps not. In any event they halted in the little triangle outside the church to speak to a passing boy. Exactly what followed has never been exactly clear. But the results are well known. Within St. Edward's the choir sang the immortal strains of the Christmas Oratorio. A golden glow from the great stained glass windows illuminated the Christmas dusk. A thousand red and green and blue lights winked from a thousand holiday homes. And a teen-age gang boy stealthily drew his switchblade knife, thrust it into the back of a sailor and ran off, leaving the man to die in a bloody pool beside the white statue of the Virgin in the churchyard.

Nor is this the only terror which has been seen from the windows looking down on St. Edward's. Here one evening there was a swift rush of children in the street, the shout of young voices, the flash of steel, the crunch of heavy boots in soft flesh. It was over in a minute. But when the youngsters fled down the street they left a boy behind them, stomped to death on St. Edward's steps.

Must these things happen? Is there some vicious, ingrained trait inherent in the people who live at Fort Greene? Not by any means.

None of the residents of these houses were born to crime— unless you count poverty, illiteracy and cultural deprivation as crimes.

The only real criminals are the men who turned Fort Greene and its sister projects into evil things.

Not all low-cost housing projects are like Fort Greene. Some are as good as you could wish. All have been founded in noble and high intent. But in practice Fort Greene and some others have been turned into monsters, devouring their residents, polluting the areas around them, spewing out a social excrescence which infects the whole of our society. The damage is not confined to New York. The violence loosed by Fort Greene sets in motion a wave of adolescent conflict which is borne from one end of the nation to the other.

Admission to low-rent projects, in New York City, basically is determined by income levels. The lower the income the higher the priority. Charity, welfare and relief cases get first choice. No discrimination for color, creed or race is permitted. Or such is the pleasant theory. Actually, the sharp knife of poverty discriminates far more effectively than a *numerus clausus*. The rules tend to make ghettos of color and race out of the huge aggregates in which one family out of twenty in New York City now lives.

In the last seven years 300,000 Puerto Ricans have migrated to New York. In the same period perhaps 300,000 Negroes have come in. A high percentage of these people are in the bottom income category. Many are jobless. They go on welfare. The transition from the barrios of Puerto Rico to the factories of New York is not always so easy.

Because of their social and economic need these people receive preference in public housing. There is nothing wrong about this. Public housing is subsidized by the state for the specific purpose of helping low-income groups. But indiscriminate application of this means test populates Fort Greene or Red Hook almost exclusively with that segment of the population which is least capable of caring for itself—economically, socially, culturally.

The concentration of the ill, the halt and the crippled (socially or physically) increases constantly because when a family's income rises to a minimum figure it must leave the project. The able, rising families are driven out month after month as their wages cross the ceiling mark. At the intake end economic and social levels drop lower and lower as inflation waters down the fixed-income limit and depression bites away at employment. It is the new unskilled immigrant from Mississipppi or San Juan who first loses his job, goes on relief and is put at the top of the waiting list for low-cost housing.

In some New York housing projects the majority of the families are welfare cases. At Red Hook Houses relief cases constitute 25 per cent of the twenty-nine hundred families in the project. By screening the applicants to eliminate those with even modest wages the project community is systematically deprived of the normal quota of human talents needed for self-organization, self-discipline and self-improvement. It becomes a catch basin for the dregs of society. It lacks capability to help itself. It breeds endless social ills. It constitutes an ever-replenishing vessel for trouble. It is a built-in consumer of limitless social assistance.

The trouble starts long before the prisonlike towers and blocks of Fort Greene or Marcy Houses begin to fill up with socially deprived people. It starts when slum clearance begins.

The stated objective of slum clearance is to clean out a section of the city which has decayed, to tear down dilapidated, rat-infested tenements, to wipe out the debris-filled "home" workshops, obliterate the dives, the dens, the cribs and the blind pigs.

The concept is a little like that of a dentist. Drill out the infected cavity and fill it with nice new wholesome cement. It may hurt a little at first but the end justifies the pain. However, the slum clearer is not a dentist. His drill uproots all the people in the neighborhood, good as well as bad. He tears down the churches. He destroys local business. He sends the neighborhood lawyer to new offices downtown. The clinic and the synagogue move to the Bronx.

Bulldozers do not understand that a community is more than broken-down buildings and dirty storefronts. It is a tight skein of human relations. It has a life all its own. The wreckers tear this human fabric to ribbons. The old-timers are driven from their run-down flats and their ancient brick houses. They cannot wait three years for the new houses to open. Nothing more than a passing effort is made to give them a place in the new building anyway. They need a place to live here and now. So they drift away. They find a worse flat in a tumble-down on the edge of the new ghetto-to-be. They go their way, resentful, bitter, lives twisted out of joint. The new neighborhood can never be as good as the old, or so they think.

The trucks begin to bring in the steel girders and the cheap brick. The new barracks go up and up. Perhaps twenty stories. (Our new slums are skyscraper slums complete with elevators. No more old-fashioned six-flight walkups.) The old-timers watch the towers rise.

"The first thing that happens," a housing man told me, "is the kids begin to destroy the property. Even before it is built. They steal the place blind. As soon as the windows go in they smash them. They smash them again and again. What difference does it make, it's public, ain't it? That's what they say."

Maybe this is just kid hooliganism. Maybe it is the kids

acting out the real feelings of the neighborhood against the new Goliath erected in their midst.

Before a single family has moved into the project the lines of community warfare have been drawn. The stage is set for hatred, feuds, gangs, rumbles, street fighting and killings.

Into this neighborhood where nerves are still raw and bleeding pour hundreds and thousands of new faces, often of a race and nationality different from that which lived there before.

This is a human revolution. But seldom are the social effects recognized. No effort is made to orient the new people. Nothing is done with the old residents. Institutions which might have been bridges between new and old have been ruthlessly ripped out.

"Wherever you have great population mobility and disrupted population areas," according to Hugh Johnson of the Youth Board, "gangs spring up to replace the broken stability of the group. Wherever the pattern of life breaks down kids form gangs to give themselves a feeling of protection and stability."

Before East Harlem began to resound to the deadly plong of the wreckers' ball and the tattoo of new steel work it was a slum. But it had many institutions that gave stability. There were the Neapolitan blocks, the street fiestas, the interwoven relationship of stores and neighbors. Out it all went. In came the gangs.

The new project may permit a church to survive on a small island like St. Edward's. But an absence of churches and an absence of religious influence is notable among project youngsters. The Negro children seldom go to church. The same is true of the Puerto Ricans. The Irish and Italian gang youngsters are usually described by their priests as "bad Catholics," irregular in church observance.

The projects are political deserts. The precinct bosses have been wiped out with the slum. They do not seem to come back. No one cares whether the new residents vote or not. There is no basket at Thanksgiving. No boss to fix it up when Jerry gets into trouble with the police. The residents have no organization of their own and are discouraged from having any.

"We don't want none of them organizers in here," one manager of a project told me. "All they do is stir up trouble. Used to be some organizers around here. But we cleaned them out good. Lotsa Communists. That's what they were."

Lack of political and social organization was not characteristic of low-rent projects when they first started going up in the late 1930's. Housing specialists understood that if you simply built barracks for the poor you were only creating a new ghetto. In the early days the housing projects had good social components.

Long before the old slum was torn down social service teams went in to prepare the people for what lay ahead. They arranged to give displaced persons priority in the new buildings. Care was taken to provide social facilities to replace those torn out. Community centers, child care centers, playgrounds and other facilities were built. (But never as many as were needed because of shortage of money.) It was recognized that families of low cultural background would have to be helped to adjust or they might turn their new surroundings into a replica of the old.

One simple and effective device used in the early days was the "rent girl." The young woman was, in fact, a social service worker or student. Each month she went from door to door and collected the rent. She stopped in for a cup of coffee or tea. She knew all the women. She knew their troubles. She was regarded as a friend—not an inquisitive social worker. She was able to help new families get started and stop trouble before it became serious. She could tell the manager what his tenants were up to. It was an effective device. It was cheap. It was simple.

But bureaucratization set in, economy waves, reduction of everything to the lowest possible denominator. It was always easy to cut the social services. They weren't essential. They were the "frills" seized on by real estate interests, stupid congressmen, sensation-mongering tabloid newspapers. The "rent girls" quickly vanished. Now, the tenant is required to come to the manager's office to pay his rent. The relationship is strictly impersonal. No one steps foot in the apartment until after the trouble starts. No one has any way of learning what is happening to the people. No one really cares.

In the early days the projects had tenants' associations. They were lively affairs, full of politics, sprouting with good works, enthusiasm and argument. They were training grounds in democracy. Then the Communists moved in on them. Soon the associations were devoting more time to the party line than to the lives of the people.

Now they have been destroyed, root and branch. Most of them found their way onto the Attorney General's subversive list. They were harassed and harried out of existence. But the destruction of the associations created a vacuum. We threw the baby out with the bath water. The big low-cost projects have no organizations, no political interests. Their community structure has been turned into social mush by stupidity and bureaucracy.

There is a "Tenants' Guild" at one project which epitomizes the level to which organization has sunk. Mrs. George Washington Astor is the leader of this guild. She told me about her work after dropping her 250-pound bulk into a plush armchair and sighing heavily.

The project has a population of more than fifteen thousand. There are eighteen members of the guild.

"Seems I never can get things done with the children running around the house," Mrs. Astor told me. I could understand that. There are seventeen persons living in a four-room flat. Ten are her own children. Four are the children of her oldest daughter, Ruby, just turned twenty-one. Ruby is not married. Each of her children has a different father. Who the other residents were I could not get clear.

"Seems as though it's hard to get the parents interested in their children 'cept when they're in trouble," Mrs. Astor said. "People like their children. But just seems though they don't never have time to go to meetings or take an interest somehow."

Mrs. Astor has been trying to get sewing classes started for the girls. "Don't know why it is," she said. "But the girls jus' don't seem to be interested."

The same fate has overtaken another project that she tried very hard to start—a girls' volleyball team.

"I must confess," Mrs. Astor said, "that membership in our guild—it isn't a club, it's a guild—has been falling off lately. One thing we did do. We had a mighty fine ball last year."

Mrs. Astor is not a figure toward whom I would direct criticism. It is not her fault that her ability and energy are limited. She is doing the best she can under many personal handicaps. The address for the direction of criticism is to those officials whose interest is so slight that they extend no helping hand to Mrs. Astor and the others like her.

The residents of some projects even find the neighborhood centers supposedly installed for their benefit closed to their use. It is usually the children who are barred from these facilities. Some centers close their doors to all youngsters except members of one designated gang. I was told of one center where until recently no children of the project it was intended to serve were being admitted. Too destructive. We must protect our property, the director insisted.

The manager of a project spoke to me in similar terms.

"My first concern is to run the project and maintain it as well as possible," he said. "I must protect the property and concern myself with vandalism, which results when youngsters don't behave. Delinquency, as I see it, is primarily van-

dalism. As far as the gangs are concerned they should be
broken up by the Police Department at every opportunity."

I asked him what he thought was the cause of gangs.

"Well," he said, thinking a bit. "I suppose it is a feeling of
wanting to belong. Some of them join to protect themselves.
Yes. Protection and wanting to belong. These are the main
things."

It was his ironclad practice that the family of any boy
found to be a gang member was given an eviction notice.
Kick 'em out! This was his rule.

It does not require much insight to see that when housing
projects are conducted in this atmosphere they contribute
to the development of gang delinquency. Ralph Whelan,
director of the New York City Youth Board, reports that his
experience shows an invariable rise in delinquency rates in
the first six to eighteen months of any new housing project.

The Chicago sociologist, Frederic M. Thrasher, attributes
this to the creation of what he calls "interstitial areas," lacings
of different ethnic and social groups which generate conflict
and the emergence of gangs.

Color seems to play only a secondary role in these conflicts.
The experience of the Riis Community Center in Red Hook
demonstrates this. Walter J. Weinert has been director there
for many years. He has watched the changing ethnic character
of the neighborhood and the shifting lines of conflict.

Before Red Hook Houses were built about twenty years
ago this was an Irish-Italian neighborhood with a long record
of combat among street gangs of the same ethnic composition.
The first tenants of Red Hook Houses were mostly Jewish.
Conflict broke out between the native Irish and Italians and
the incoming Jewish residents. Hostility was common among
adults. There was gang fighting between the adolescents.

The population of Red Hook Houses today is two-thirds
Negro and Puerto Rican. The hostility between project and
neighborhood has not lessened. Ethnic lines have changed.

Lines of combat have not. From the social standpoint the Red Hook neighborhood is more fortunate than others. It has a well-run community center, street club workers provided by the Youth Board and a Catholic Youth Center. But today, twenty years after the establishment of the Housing Project, there are only rudimentary beginnings of an organization designed to integrate the project and the community. Even this effort to lessen hostility would not have been made but for the initiative of the Youth Board.

The mere fact that a housing project has existed in a community for many years is no guarantee of lack of tension. The population within the project shifts constantly. Residents are forced out because their income goes over the permitted maximum or because of misconduct, usually gang activity by the children. The evictees often find slum housing in the same area. Their bitterness at eviction adds to the cumulative total of bitterness.

Yet, none of this need be.

There are excellent examples of low-cost housing in many parts of the United States—housing accompanied by thoughtful, effective social planning which gets the best results from the expenditure of public funds. Such planning strengthens the community rather than weakens it. In a real sense this is urban renewal so badly needed by our many blighted cities. Such good projects can be found in Stamford and New Haven, Connecticut. They can be seen in Newark, New Jersey, just across the Hudson River from New York in a city which has the same metropolitan problems as Manhattan. But in Newark there are intelligent and sensitive officials, interested not just in payrolls but in the improvement of the community. They demonstrate clearly that it is not the system but the way it is run which makes the difference.

Indeed, New York itself has some good low-income housing. One of the best projects exists in Chelsea on the lower West Side. Credit for this goes mostly to the social understanding and vigor of the Hudson Guild, a settlement house founded by the late Dr. John Lovejoy Elliott in 1895.

Until just before World War II Chelsea had been a comfortable lower-middle-class and workingman's residential neighborhood, largely Irish and Italian. Many men drove trucks or worked on the nearby docks. It was a close-knit community. Everyone knew whose boy married whose girl. It was a good place for kids to grow up in. There was credit at the grocery store when a man had to lay off work with a strained back. Rents were cheap, housing not too bad, the schools were good and there was a hospital nearby.

But the housing began to run down and a project was built in the area, opening in 1947. Veterans were given preference. The income requirements were low and few of the displaced residents of Chelsea were able to get flats in the new houses. Hostility to the project ran high. It mounted higher when it was learned that Negroes would be admitted to Elliott Houses. There was talk of going into the streets to prevent the Negro invasion.

At this point Hudson Guild went into action. It undertook to explain to every family in the whole community just what the Project was and what it would do for the area and why the new residents should be welcomed. The job was done well. One of the first Negro families was refused admission to Elliott Houses after the moving truck with their furniture had arrived. It was a technical difficulty of some kind. But Chelsea didn't know that. The whole community stormed over to the project office, demanding that the Negro family be permitted to move in.

Dan Carpenter and Tom Wolfe, leaders of Hudson Guild, knew that this was only one side of the coin. The other was the task of fitting the newcomers into the community. Six hundred and seven families moved in, forty-seven of them Negro.

"We set up a model apartment," Wolfe recalls. "We showed

the new people how to furnish their apartments. We explained about time payments and how they could buy second-hand furniture much cheaper and fix it up with a little paint. We visited every family as it came in. We told them all about their new community."

The results can be imagined. Elliott Houses became part of the Chelsea community. There was no dividing line between new and old. Rather, a firm new bond was created and one which was quickly needed. Without the sound early work at Elliott Houses, Chelsea would have become a street battleground when hundreds of Puerto Rican families began to pour into the area. Chelsea had absorbed some three thousand Negroes without undue tension but the flood of Puerto Ricans caused trouble. It shifted the population balance radically. There are perhaps twenty-five thousand Puerto Ricans now in a total of sixty-five thousand population. Most of the Puerto Ricans have come in the last five years.

Street gangs appeared in Chelsea, but by strenuous work the Hudson Guild contained the situation. It put a large Spanish-language program into action. It managed to prevent the development of chronic street war and, instead, channeled the clubs into social activities.

Meantime, the ethnic composition of Elliott Houses has shifted. It is now roughly one-third Negro, one-third Puerto Rican, and one-third white.

"And that is the way we want it to stay," the Hudson Guild people say. They are tough about this point. They won't listen to the arguments of purists who insist that they must not tamper with "natural" selection.

"We believe in this neighborhood," Mr. Wolfe says. "We believe in it being a good place for people to live. If we can maintain the housing project on its present balance we can hold the line of the community."

A big union co-op housing project is coming into the area.

This will bring in about twenty-six hundred middle-income families. It will balance the middle-income loss that has been suffered due to the Puerto Rican influx. (For example, St. Columba parish lost two hundred of its sixteen hundred families, mostly middle-income, last year. They moved out of the parish.)

"We don't want any ghettos here," Mr. Wolfe says. "We want a comfortable neighborhood in which everyone can live his own life decently. There is no bopping here. Our boys are growing up as good boys. And we are going to see that they have a chance to go on growing up that way."

I walked away from Hudson Guild in the bright sunshine of a brilliant New York day. The Guild is located in the center of the housing project. Sunning themselves in a tree-lined courtyard were old men reading their papers and young mothers with their perambulators. On the street leading away from Elliott Houses a half-dozen teen-agers were playing bounce ball against a wall. Two were Negro, two Puerto Rican and two white. They seemed to be having a good time. No shifty glances from the corners of their eyes, no telltale movements of hands toward switchblades hidden in trousers pockets. They didn't even bother to look up when I went past. I thought they seemed relaxed and secure. It was a good sight to see on the streets of New York City—the kind of a sight which with some expenditure of thought, energy and money could be made too common to be worthy of mention.

6

the old slums

THE first thing that struck me about Forsyth Street was that most of the clocks were an hour slow. They hadn't bothered to change to summer time. Apparently an hour didn't make that much difference there.

Forsyth Street is a short lane in the heart of the old East Side. It begins where Chinatown comes to an end at the Manhattan Bridge Plaza and passes across Rivington Street, Grand Street, Broome Street and Delancey Street. In the America in which I grew up those names were synonymous with poverty, deprivation, exploitation. They reeked of the sweatshop, the white plague, vice and misery. Today the names are forgotten. The schoolchildren of Kansas City, Atlanta and Seattle are not stirred by stories of the "melting pot." The great crusades for wiping the shame of the slums from the bright escutcheon of democracy have long been forgotten. Ellis Island is an unwanted piece of real estate on the auction block. No one even thinks of making it a monument to the millions who paused on its soil. Outside the narrow circle of professional social work few remember Jacob Riis, Lillian Wald, Lincoln Steffens or Edward Bok. The spirit of the muckrakers has been scientifically homogenized into the pablum of the Organization Man.

The slums? Oh, they have vanished. We have obliterated them with ready-mixed concrete and super-highways, with asphalt vistas and steel towers. So we suppose. So I, too, supposed until a few months ago when I got acquainted with Forsyth Street. Someone had told me that a good many Puerto Rican families were moving into the old East Side slums and that I would find a small Catholic mission on Forsyth Street which was working with these families. Since the Puerto Ricans are blamed by many persons for generating much of the delinquency and adolescent street warfare in the city I thought it would be worth while to pay a call at the mission.

I had not walked very far down Forsyth Street before my naïve assumptions about the "old slums" began to vanish. Some characteristics of a former day persisted at the Williamsburg Bridge end of the street. Once, apparently, this had been a center for cheap, sweated jewelry manufacture. Here had congregated emigrants from the ghettos of eastern Europe. Many were skilled in the lapidary arts. Others worked in precious metals. Here they set up their side-street shops and hole-in-the-wall artels. Long since the industry has moved away from Forsyth Street. But a remnant remains. A manufacturing jeweler's sign in a grime-covered window. A silver plating establishment. A diamond setter. Retail and wholesale jewelry businesses. It was in these stores that so many of the clocks remained on standard time.

Deeper into Forsyth Street its character subtly changes. I watched a blind Chinese, a wizened old man with a white cane, tap, tap, tap along the sidewalk. A Negro with scarred face, dungarees and glazed eyes passed me, lurching a little. A slight velvet-collared man with olive face scuttled into a doorway, his arm around the narrow waist of a thin, dark-haired girl.

Delancey Street is broad and traffic-filled. Two officers were directing a heavy flow of trucks. This is the site of a big sub-way extension project. It looked as though a blockbuster had fallen. On the corner the sagging skeleton of an old tenement. Rubble piles where other buildings used to stand. Barricades around a crater that once was a park.

Across Delancey Street the neighborhood grows worse. The stores bear Spanish names. Bodegas replace kosher markets. Here a young Puerto Rican with white shirt, open at the neck, sits on the iron stoop of an old house. He strums his guitar thoughtfully. On the other steps sit four girls and a little boy. A woman stands in the doorway and listens. Here is the brick façade and the iron-barred gates of Public School No. 91. Beside the curb eight garbage cans await the pickup. On the school steps drowses a powerfully built old man, his hand holding up a chin covered with quarter-inch, iron-gray stubble. Here is the darkened window of a store-front church with its name in white paint: "The Church of the Needed Star." Perhaps a poet preaches here.

A little further down the street is the Nativity Mission Center of Father Walter Janer and Father John G. Hoodak, located in a narrow old tenement, the upper floors of which are given over to a small convent. Father Janer was born and raised in Puerto Rico. Father Hoodak is of Ukranian origin. No persons know better than they the new life of the old slums. Father Janer founded this mission ten years ago when the first Puerto Rican families began to come in. Ten years ago the old slum was withering away. Restricted immigration from Europe, the movement of second-generation families to more attractive parts of the city, the steady encroachment of housing projects and slum clearance schemes had apparently sounded the death knell for the old East Side. Ten years ago the image in my mind of the vanishing slum was valid. Then came the influx of new Puerto Rican and Negro populations. They needed cheap places to live. The old slums went back into business. Abandoned tenements were reopened. The squalor of a generation or two ago began to return. It was the same old story. Only worse.

What about living conditions in the new-old slums, I asked Father Hoodak.

"There is only one word for them—intolerable," he said, biting it off short.

Although city officials still classify the area of Forsyth Street as an Italian-Jewish neighborhood it has twenty-seven different nationalities. Among them are seventy thousand Puerto Ricans. Most of the Puerto Ricans are young people. Seven out of eight are under forty years old. Almost half are children.

I have visited the places where these families live. These are not tenements. They are the dregs of tenements. A hundred years ago they were accurately described by Charles Dickens. Indeed, he may have had some of these very places in mind when he wrote:

"What place is this to which the squalid street conducts us? A kind of square of leprous houses, some of which are attainable only by crazy wooden stairs without. What lies beyond this tottering flight of steps that creak beneath our tread—a miserable room, lighted by one candle and destitute of all comfort save that which may be hidden in a wretched bed. . . ."

The newly arrived Puerto Ricans are unfamiliar with city ways. They are cheated and robbed without mercy. A fifteen-by-twenty room in a hundred-year-old house is rented to a family of four for twenty dollars a week. Slightly smaller rooms cost fifteen dollars. There is no water. Little heat in winter. A gas plate for cooking. No refrigerator. No icebox. No bath. No shower. A dirty toilet and a single faucet down the hall. I went into one house of three stories. There were six cubicles to a floor. By renting each at $15 a week the thieving landlord was taking more than $1,000 a month out of a rat-infested building in which a farmer would not think of housing goats.

I asked Madame Encarnación Armas, a Puerto Rican woman who is devoting herself to politics, what were the agencies which took an interest in newly arriving Puerto Ricans.

"A good question," she said. "I'll tell you who takes an interest in the Puerto Rican—the owner of the cheap rooming house who is getting rich off a building that should be condemned and torn down. The cheap furniture dealer who sells junk on the installment plan. The dealer who cashes pay checks and sells wine and whiskey. The loft proprietor and the fly-by-night who employ the Puerto Rican at a fraction of the union scale. Oh, yes, there are many, many people in New York who take a very personal interest in the Puerto Rican."

The Puerto Ricans and the new arrivals from the Deep South constitute the current generation of greenhorns—fair prey for all the sharp and cynical doubledealers of the big city.

"Walk down our streets of a summer evening," Father Hoodak said, "say at eleven or twelve o'clock. You will see little children three and four years old sitting on the stoops or playing under the lights. Why are they on the streets? A very simple reason. They can't go to bed. Someone is sitting on it. Until the adults are ready for bed there is no place for the children to sleep."

The children have no privacy. There is no place for them to study. You may see them at night with their books open in the game room of a neighborhood center. It is more quiet there than at home. They never live long in one spot. Two-thirds of the families in this area have applications in for low-rent housing flats. There is a 60 to 70 per cent turnover each year at Nativity Mission. Look at the records of these youngsters in school. They have lived at fifteen addresses in the last two or three years. They are birds of passage, rootless and drifting, pathetic examples to buttress the conviction of Albert Schweitzer that "modern man is lost in the mass in a way which is without precedent in history."

Here are all the social evils of the great city which most of us comfortably living middle-class Americans thought had long since been relegated to the annals of the past.

In front of the Nativity Mission and occupying the hundred feet which separate Forsyth and Chrystie streets is a long narrow park, designed as a play area for slum children. It bears the honored name of Sara Delano Roosevelt. The concept was praiseworthy, but like so many of the city's efforts it took little heed of reality. The upper end of the park lies close to the Bowery, still the same old street of lost men. The "Bowery Boys," derelicts of humanity, living on alms and cheap alcohol, have pre-empted half of the children's park. On the long summer days they sun themselves and drowse away the rotgut whiskey which helps them forget the world which they unfortunately cannot leave. No storytellers for children visit this grim greensward. No Hans Christian Andersen figures decorate the playground.

"Every kind of vice you can think of goes on in that park," Father Hoodak said. "I cannot bring myself to tell you what goes on."

Amidst it all the children play. Where else can they go? The lower half of the park which they used to use is now the crater of the great subway project.

"This is so typical of city bureaucracy," Father Hoodak said. "The children's only place has been torn up. Nothing is done to provide a new playground. The city owns a parking lot around the corner which would do nicely. There is talk about making it available. But nothing happens. And another hot summer lies ahead."

But children are clever. If there is no place to play they will make one. This has happened on Forsyth Street. Not long ago the subway construction chief asked Father Janer to stop by. He thought the father might help with a problem. He led the father to the edge of the great crater, an excavation that goes down seventy or eighty feet. The hole has been filled with a crisscross of steel beams and uprights, the supports for the subway and the new station. The area is surrounded by a tight board fence. Armed, uniformed guards patrol it.

"Look, Father," the perspiring construction boss said. "I've offered anything to get them to stay out—uniforms, bus trips, baseball, Cokes. Whatever they want, I'll get it, believe me. But they pay no attention."

Father Janer looked into the great hole. Here were dozens of children, some only eight or nine years old, playing tag in the steel framework. To them it seemed as though the new steel structure was just a giant "jungle" like the bars and cages of their vanished playground. They raced about the narrow girders, clambered up and down, oblivious of danger. And always just out of reach of guards and workmen. They greeted Father Janer gaily.

"I'll go away soon," one boy shouted. "Just as soon as I'm through playing. We'll all go home in an hour."

"What can we do?" Father Janer asked. "It is incredibly dangerous. They don't understand that at all. Sooner or later one of them is going to fall and break his neck. But how can we stop them? They don't know the difference between good and bad, between good behavior and bad behavior. No one teaches them. Authority means nothing—except something to rebel against."

There are perils even worse than the seventy-foot excavation in and around Forsyth Street. This is an area of much narcotics traffic. It is known for its "pushers" (dope salesmen) and "junkies" (addicts). It is also known for wholesale trade, establishments devoted to the manufacture and "cutting" or dilution of narcotics for street sale. Federal and city authorities are active. So is the traffic.

"Yesterday," said Father Hoodak, "I saw a twelve-year-old girl hanging out in a candy store near here. I know that dope users hang out there. She is a good girl and she comes from a good family."

Father Hoodak sought out the girl later and asked why she went to the place. She said her mother was working and she had no place to go during the lunch hour.

"I asked her if she didn't know it was a bad place where they used dope. She said she didn't know."

"Somebody put some sneezing powder under my nose," the girl told Father Hoodak. Sneezing powder is heroin.*

The vice business is an ally of the dope business. The two go hand in hand. First the girl is "hooked" to drugs. Then, she is put into prostitution to earn money to pay for her drugs.

The easiest age at which an addict is created is teen-age. The teen-ager lacks judgment, is heedless of risks, ready to experiment.

The area near Forsyth Street is a recruiting grounds for young prostitutes. The pushers and the pimps work hand in hand. Often they combine their roles.

Only a few days before I met Father Janer he had been called in to try to save a girl from the first steps on this familiar path. The girl was fifteen. Her older brother was trying to look out for her. He came to Father Janer for assistance.

"Please," he said, "I need help with Rosa. She is getting more and more wild. I can't do anything with her. Something bad is going to happen if I don't get her out of the neighborhood. An older man is after her. He is a bad man. So far nothing bad has happened. But it will if she goes on living at home."

* Police later raided this place.

Father Janer called one social agency after another. He called seven in all. No, each said. We can't take her. Nothing has happened. There are no grounds. No, we are too crowded. No, our rules do not permit. No, such cases should stay at home.

Father Janer gave up. He could think of no other place to call. A week later it happened. Just as the brother feared. The girl ran off with the older man. Now, everything changed. Now the police moved in. The girl was found. The courts were ready to commit her to an institution. The agencies were ready to take her.

But first, she must fall into delinquency. Only damaged goods need apply.

Still, Rosa's fate is better than that of many girls in this area—girls without brothers to notify the police, girls who are firmly hooked onto drugs and condemned to a life of cheap prostitution.

Dope is not the only illicit product of the neighborhood. This is also an area of moonshine whiskey, cheap synthetic liquor made from industrial alcohol in tenement back rooms and sold in plain jugs for Friday-night parties and weekend jags. The Puerto Ricans buy it. It is cheap. And there is a big market among the Bowery boys. Sometimes, the maker is careless or ignorant. Then his customers may die. In one case up in East Harlem this year more than twenty persons died from drinking a bootleg product made from the wrong kind of stolen industrial alcohol.

Even in the best of circumstances it would not be easy for the Puerto Rican to adjust to American conditions and the American way of life. In Puerto Rico, as Emily Weinman noted in her master's thesis for the New York School of Social Work, "the family is the most important social institution in the lives of the people." The male is the unquestioned boss of the home, the breadwinner, the dominant figure. Women usually are not wage earners. They devote themselves to the children. Children are highly regarded and overprotected. Love and affection are heaped on them. They are an economic asset, bringing more to the family by their labor than is expended for their food and clothing. There are many common-law marriages in sugar-cane communities but these relationships are firm and enduring. Puerto Rican children play happily and naturally.

Delinquency was unknown until very, very recently. Now it is beginning to spread as a re-export from America. Returning families and children bring "American" cultural patterns back to the tranquil island. Gangs are springing up. The impact of industrial civilization and industrial mores, mass consumers' goods and mass consumers' wants are putting new stress on the agrarian culture of Puerto Rico.

The incoming Puerto Rican family in America must adjust to radical change in every sphere. The woman gets better pay than her husband. She works in the needle trades. He becomes a janitor, a messenger, a pearl diver in a restaurant. His jobs are menial, ill paid. No longer does the woman look to the man for protection. He is in second place. The woman does not have to obey. Even in the best families there are internal strains.

Outside the home there are hostility and conflict. A Puerto Rican woman of culture told me how she and her husband had moved into a good Irish residential neighborhood in Brooklyn. One day soon after they moved into the neighborhood, boys attacked her son. The second time this happened she complained to the precinct police.

"Why did you move into this area?" the desk sergeant asked. "What do you expect?" The boy was beaten again. He was hit over the eye with a brick. The wound required several stitches. Boys came to the door of the house, rang the bell and shouted: "If you don't move we will wreck your house." The next day they left dead cats on the porch. Only when the woman made plain to the police that she would go to City Hall—and that she knew someone to go to—did they send around a policeman. After that the terrorism ended. It was not long before the Puerto Rican youngster and his Irish neighbors became good friends.

Not many Puerto Ricans who move into Forsyth Street know what to do with their problems. They expect little from the police although this happens to be a good precinct from the Puerto Rican viewpoint, possibly because there is a Puerto Rican officer on the staff. Some Puerto Rican problems are created by the ignorance of the bureaucracy. For instance, Puerto Ricans love children. This is one of their most enviable characteristics. If a neighbor cannot bring up a child they freely take the youngster into their family and bring it up as their own. There is no difference in treatment between a *hijo de ciranza,* a "bringing-up child," and their own. But such a relationship is too complex for many Welfare Department clerks to understand. Even the Puerto Rican system of names, the use of both the mother's and father's names, causes endless complication. Petty officials often treat common-law marriages as though they constituted gross immorality. They have caused the separation of husbands and wives who have lived in common-law wedlock for years.

These are the kind of tangles that Father Janer and Father Hoodak spend day after day in untangling. And who but these middle-aged priests would have the time and affection on Forsyth Street to look after Chico, ten years old, eyes like black buttons, and once called the worst problem child of the year at P.S. No. 91?

"Chico had a dossier two inches thick before the principal called up and asked whether we would try a hand with him," Father Hoodak laughed. Once when Chico threw a temper tantrum it took half a dozen teachers to subdue his wiry little frame. But you'd never believe it when he comes hop-skipping into Father Hoodak's two-by-four office with an air of innocent anticipation. Chico has no father. His mother works. They live with an aunt and uncle.

"There's nothing the matter with Chico that a little love won't cure," Father Hoodak said. "Sure, I suppose I'm what a psychologist would call a father image in his life. Whatever I am, he's stopped being a problem at P.S. No. 91."

There is no social agency in New York which gets along on a smaller budget than the Nativity Mission Center. It manages to operate on less than $20,000 a year. "We operate on less than a businessman charges off in a year for luncheon expenses," Father Janer says. Father Hoodak keeps the petty cash in a small canvas bag in his desk. It often contains nothing but pennies and nickels. When he buys candy bars for the kids he goes two blocks out of the way to get them ten cents a dozen cheaper. There is nothing fancy about the mission's program. If your biggest room is forty by twenty-five feet and you have only four or five rooms in all you can't go in for volleyball, amateur dramatics or eurythmic dancing. But penny bingo is fun for the kids of Forsyth Street even though it may not be listed in the social service manuals, and it keeps fifty or sixty youngsters out of mischief every Friday afternoon. On Forsyth Street that is an achievement. One way or another the center manages to look after 500 or more kids every year. The Fathers handle more than 1,000 adult cases, too—400 couples with marital problems, 250 mothers with children's problems, a couple of hundred relief and health cases and too many others to list. Nativity Mission Center is a busy and wonderful place. Fortunately, it is only one of a wealth of resources which the old slum commands.

There is no area of New York City with so high a concentration of social services. The slums of Chicago, San Francisco and Los Angeles have nothing to compare with the fine social facilities built up in the long immigrant years. Most of them still remained when the new population movement began. This is unlike the pattern in some sections of the city where facilities, closely tied with ethnic, national or religious groups, moved out along with the outward exodus of the older slum residents. In the lower East Side you find such organizations as University Settlement House, the famous Henry Street Settlement House founded by Lillian Wald, the Educational Alliance, the fine programs of Trinity Episcopal parish, the selfless charities of Dorothy Day and the *Catholic Worker* and many others.

The newer slums like Bedford-Stuyvesant never developed a network of social agencies and many raw new housing projects, rammed into blighted regions, are completely devoid of facilities. Thus, the old slum affords some advantages over the new.

"Even a ghetto, after it has remained a ghetto over a period of time," the Rev. Jerry Oniki of the Church of the Master in Harlem pointed out, "builds up its social structure, and this makes for more stability, more leadership, more agencies for helping the solution of public problems."

There are shallow critics who believe that the lower East Side has too high a concentration of settlement houses. Anyone who has seen conditions there can only suppose that this suggestion comes from those who believe that the cure for poverty is to spread your penury even thinner than it is already.

Not even the concentration of social agencies in the old East Side slums has been able to prevent the emergence of adolescent gangs and teen-age delinquency. The newly arrived Puerto Ricans and Negroes are forced almost automatically into street conflict with the Italians and Jews already living in the slum. They react in a predictable pattern.

"You must remember," Mr. Oniki said, "that these are peasant children for the most part. They differ in many ways from middle-class youngsters. Swearing is normal behavior for them. But when they bring this language into school it shocks the middle-class teacher. Sex knowledge is more advanced, direct and primitive in these classes. Here, too, a conflict with the middle-class mores of the city emerges. The peasant class is not so articulate, not so verbal as the middle class. It is more accustomed to resolving problems by physical action or physical violence."

For youngsters who are the products of such a background the road to violent gang action and all its antisocial consequences is short and straight. They band together for physical protection and as their strength increases quickly shift over to aggression. They have no value structure or if they do it is one based on the law of force, the law of the old slum.

The Forsyth Street area is a reception center for the arriving Puerto Ricans and Negroes. For most families it is their first haven on entering a strange and bewildering city. These are the streets where thousands of youngsters make their first acquaintance with the superior culture and advanced civilization of America's finest city. From here they move to other areas of the city and spread out over the whole country firmly infected with the poisons of group hostility and the mores of the street gang. They do not feel that there is anything wrong with the gang and its mores. Indeed, in the milieu of Forsyth Street the structural development and quasi-institutionalized form of the gang almost appears as a superior form of social organization. In a desert even a flask of muddy water tastes sweet.

The transition of a peasant society to an industrial civilization is never accomplished without blood and tears. Considering the actual content of the life to which the new arrivals are subjugated there can be little wonder that the adolescents are badly shaken. If a rich city permits a gangrenous ulcer like Forsyth Street to exist it should at least have the grace to cease pretending that the revolt of the adolescents is an imported product. No one who visits Forsyth Street can fail to perceive that our shook-up generation bears a made-in-America label. Other countries subject their youth to cruel and unusual strains and stresses. But we need take no back seat. The clocks in Forsyth Street may run an hour late but the forces of social disintegration are operating on an overtime basis.

7

the suburbs

THE two boys were a little tight when they came out of Freddy's Bar & Grill and got into the new cream-and-green Buick sedan. It was spring vacation and both were home in South Neck from college. Roy was a junior at Union College and Ralph was a sophomore at Cornell. Roy was twenty; Ralph, nineteen.

"You're sure she'll have a friend," Ralph asked nervously as Roy started the car.

"She better, the black bitch," the older boy said. "If she doesn't you can have her when I'm through."

The boys drove in silence through the spring evening. South Neck is a rather large suburb of New York, about forty-five minutes' ride from Grand Central. Twenty years ago it was quite exclusive. Today it is predominantly middle-class and upper middle-class. Most housewives in South Neck do their own work with the aid of a girl once or twice a week. These domestic workers are Negroes for the most part. Lately, more and more have been young girls, some still in their teens, newly arrived from Florida and Georgia. These girls, new to the North, work for slightly lower wages until they learn the ropes.

Among some of the middle-class boys of the late teens and early twenties a fad has sprung up of "dating" these Negro girls. The boys pick them up, usually by prearrangement, buy them a few drinks in a highway tavern, take them to the drive-in movies or park with them in lovers' lanes. They deposit the girls at the station in time for a late train back to New York.

"It's a big thrill for the girls," one of the boys explained. "Most of them are from the South. They've never been out with a white man before. It's a kick."

The kick, it is apparent, works both ways.

When Roy and Ralph got to the meeting place only one girl, a thin, rather good-looking light tan girl of eighteen or nineteen was standing there. Her girl friend, she explained, couldn't come.

Roy turned the wheel over to Ralph and got into the back seat with the girl.

"Just drive around," he ordered. "I got business to attend to."

The girl giggled nervously. "Where's this place you said we would go to?" she asked.

"You'd be surprised," Roy said, pulling her over to him.

Later, Ralph told the boys at Freddy's what had happened.

"Geez," he said, "don't tell Roy but I was kinda scared. I didn't know what to do. They were all quiet in the back seat. Then, I heard a noise like the girl was being sick or something. Kind of a choking noise. There was a slap and I looked back and Roy was belting the hell out of her."

Ralph said he had slowed the car for a turn when he heard the door slam and the girl scream at almost the same time. He turned his head and saw that the girl was gone.

"I said, 'What happened, Roy,' and he said, 'I kicked her the hell out of the car.' I said why and he said, 'I didn't like the way she was doing it, that's all.' I asked him about the funny noise and he laughed. 'Oh, I just choked her a little to see if she'd get any better. She didn't so I threw her the hell out.' "

The South Neck police say that there have been several complaints in the last six months by Negro girls who reported that they had been assaulted by white teen-agers. One girl said she was standing on a corner waiting for a bus. A car with six white boys in it, all under twenty, pulled up beside her. A boy said: "Come on with us." The girl refused. Three boys jumped out of the car, pulled her into the rear seat and held her down. They drove to a deserted lane outside town, ripped off her clothes and raped her while one boy held a knife against her throat.

"We don't want no trouble around here," a police sergeant said. "We try to discourage them from filing complaints. This is a quiet community and we aim to keep it that way. We have some fine people here. Of course, sometimes, the kids get a little wild. But we try to keep things in the family you might say."

There have been no arrests in the assault complaints.

I asked the officer whether there were any gangs in South Neck.

"No, sir," he said. "There's none of that cowboy stuff like they have in New York. We wouldn't allow that. Not for a minute."

What, I said, about a report I had heard that a gang of Negro boys had driven down one of the main streets of town on a recent evening, firing shots in the air, and stopping to beat up two boys who were walking home from the railroad station.

That had happened, he conceded. But those "hoods" better not try it again. They'd get what they had coming. He didn't think the Negroes were from New York. Probably from Newport, a nearby suburban town with several factories and a small Negro population.

Perhaps there is no connection between the assaults on

Negro girls by the white boys of "good" family and the incursion of the Negro gang. The police think not. But there is no doubt that in a deeper sense the two phenomena are intimately linked. Both are part of the pattern of delinquency in a middle-class setting, the manifestation of the shook-up generation in the American suburb.

No subject is more difficult to analyze or even to get information on than the extent and nature of antisocial activity by the children of white-collar families, the "better class" people in medium-sized communities, the families which make up 90 per cent of the population of so many suburbs and residential developments.

It is the thesis of Dr. Walter B. Miller, director of a special research project on youth in middle-class Roxbury, Massachusetts, a suburb of Boston, that much public concern over delinquency stems not from an increase in antisocial conduct but from the fact that patterns of conduct formerly exclusive to poor, working-class or lower-middle-class youngsters, have spread to the middle-class as a whole and to upper-class youth, as well.

This, he believes, has aroused middle-class anxiety. He cites the rock 'n' roll fad as an example of how lower-class culture and speech patterns have engulfed all American youth regardless of social status.

There may be some truth in Dr. Miller's idea. But there is reason to believe that there has always been much more antisocial conduct among children of better families than is generally known, largely because these families possess the ability to conceal or wipe out the evidence of what their children do.

When twelve-year-old Peter and his friend, thirteen-year-old John, walk into Kresge's on the main street of South Neck and swipe some candy bars off the counter and are caught as they try to sneak out the manager doesn't call the police. He knows the boys. He has seen them often with their mothers

who are good customers. He bawls the kids out and sends
them home. If he is thoroughly annoyed (because children's
shoplifting goes on every day of the week) he may call up
the mothers. But he does not think of arresting the youngsters. But if the same thing happens in Bedford-Stuyvesant
and the kids are caught the policeman is called in, the kids
are dragged off to the station house, they are sent up to
Children's Court, put on probation and classified as juvenile
delinquents.

If sixteen-year-old George and three of his friends "bor-
row" a nice-looking Pontiac convertible from the country
club parking lot and set off on a joy ride and are caught
speeding by the county police they are taken to the station
house, all right, but nothing goes on the blotter. The parents
come down, there is much talk, the fathers bawl the day-
lights out of the boys, the kids promise to be good, any
damage to the car is paid for by the parents, the owner
wouldn't think of making any charge and by two o'clock in
the morning everyone is back home, peacefully sleeping. At
Christmas time the police captain gets several very nice presents. There's no case, no record, no statistics, "no delinquency."

When seventeen-year-old Joan gets pregnant after letting
eighteen-year-old Denis "fool around" at a beach party one
summer night she isn't sent to Youth House. Nor is Denis
confronted with the dilemma of marrying the girl or facing a
charge of statutory rape. There is an angry dispute between
the two families. Joan's family blames Denis. Denis's family
blames Joan. In the end Joan's father finds a doctor who takes
care of Joan for $750. Joan is a month late starting school in
the fall because, as her mother explains to the principal, she
had such a bad reaction from the antibiotics they gave her at
the camp up in New Hampshire where she went in August.

This is the classic middle-class way of dealing with the
problems of antisocial conduct which when they arise in the

slum become the bread-and-butter business of the police, the courts and the social agency.

As Professor MacIver of the New York Delinquency Evaluation Survey puts it:

"There is much more upper-class gang activity than is realized. There is more delinquency. But it is covered up. It is almost impossible to get statistics on it. We know that it exists. We know that there is much theft by middle-class children. We know there is much sex deviation. But it is all nicely covered up. A middle-class child has to act much worse than a poor boy before his conduct becomes the subject of a notation on the police blotter."

The chief of detectives of a large Middle Western city with a commendably low juvenile delinquency record says privately that he has more cases and more trouble in the district of the town's most fashionable high school than in any other section.

"It's so," he said. "But for heaven's sake don't quote me. I have enough trouble from the mothers and father already."

Does this mean that there is today more delinquency than before among children from so-called better homes? Is the middle-class component of the shook-up generation growing? I think the answer is yes to both of those questions.

The first scientific, sociological studies of this problem are just beginning to be reported. They show that the supposed immunity of "better" families to delinquency is an illusion. Albert K. Cohen, the author of classic studies on delinquency and teen-age gangs, selected a group of 337 college students, representing a cross-section of better economic and social strata. None of these youngsters had a criminal record. They were given a list of fifty-five offenses—the fifty-five for which slum children are most often arrested—and asked to check any which they had ever committed. Every boy checked at least one offense. James F. Short of the Washington State College sociology department has just completed a comprehensive study of the relationship, if any, between income, social status and delinquency.

"The traditional assumption of a higher incidence of delinquent behavior among members of the lower socio-economic group, based on official statistics, is not substantiated," he reported.

Mr. Short compared youngsters from three Western cities of ten to twenty-five thousand population with a control group in the Washington State training schools. He found virtually no difference in the incidence of delinquency. Kenneth Polk of the University of California at Los Angeles sampled San Diego youngsters and came to the same conclusion—no correlation between economic status and delinquency. This does not mean that there is not more delinquency in a slum than in a first-class residential area; that children fortunate enough to have good, warm, interested families are as subject to delinquency as those who come from broken homes; that children who play freely in open spaces are as subject to trouble as those who live on streets ruled by gangs. What it means is that neither money nor social status, per se, affords a clue to delinquency liability.

Take, for instance, what happened in Massapequa, Long Island. Massapequa is a good middle-class suburb of New York. Families move there from Manhattan to get their children away from the "bad" conditions in the New York City schools.

A few months ago two fifteen-year-old boys were living in Massapequa with their families. One boy lived with his father, manager of a New York trucking company, his mother and his twelve-year-old sister in a pleasant white Cape Cod house. The other lived in a new ranch-type house on a quiet tree-lined street with his father, a photoengraver in New York, his mother, an older brother and three younger sisters. The two houses were about three miles apart. Both boys went to Massapequa High School. Both were in ninth grade.

One day in the washroom of the school Bruce Zator, who was the boy who lived in the ranch-type house, had a fight with a boy named Butch O'Malley. The boy from the Cape Cod cottage, Timothy Wall, intervened. According to Butch Timothy knocked a knife out of Bruce's hand. Bruce, he said, warned them: "I'll get you two."

Bruce, a curly-haired, rather quiet boy, had not been doing well in his studies. He had been getting poor grades and lately had failed in two subjects. Because of this he was referred to the school psychologist. But he had never had any kind of disciplinary trouble.

About the time that Bruce and Butch had their fight in the washroom Bruce's father brought him a present from New York—a new shotgun. Bruce and his father planned to go hunting for rabbits.

For some reason, possibly because he was afraid of repercussions from his fight with Butch, Bruce stayed away from school for about five days. Finally, on a Tuesday he returned to school with his parents. On Wednesday morning Bruce got to school bright and early. By a little after eight in the morning he was in the lavatory where he had had the fight two weeks before.

According to the police Bruce went into one of the lavatory stalls. Presently Tim came into the room, went to the washbasin and started to comb his hair. A moment later, according to the story a third boy told the police, a voice rang out: "This is for you, Timmy, you creep."

Tim turned from the mirror at the sound of the voice, a gun roared, and he fell to the lavatory floor. He died a few minutes later in the school infirmary. Half an hour later police captured Bruce. He was wearing a raincoat under which, they said, he had concealed a single-barrel 12-gauge shotgun with a 12-inch stock. The barrel had been filed down to two inches.

Police charged that on the day before Bruce returned to

school he filed down the gun and provided himself with some Double-O shells. They arrested Bruce and held him on first-degree murder charges.

Both school and police officials went to some pains to emphasize that this was not a "gang" killing, that it resulted from personal differences. While it was acknowledged that there was a "club" called the Clovers at the school the authorities said this had nothing to do with the case.

This insistence on the part of the authorities seems rather facile since regardless of whether there was an organized teen-age gang in the school the whole affair was permeated with gang morals, gang tactics and gang technique. The sawed-off shotgun from the time of Al Capone and George (Bugs) Moran has been the favored weapon of gangland. And only by the intrusion of the mores of the street could a schoolboys' lavatory quarrel turn into a fatal affair. The best that could be said is that the killing of one schoolboy did not lead to a whole series of attacks as might have been the case in a street fighting area of Brooklyn.

Massapequa, unfortunately, is not the only quiet, middle-class suburb which has been shocked into awareness of the violence of which the shook-up generation is capable. Suburban communities all over the country have been building new schools at an unprecedented rate to cope with rising school populations. Repeatedly, communities which have invested hundreds of thousands or millions of dollars in new school structures have seen these fine new buildings assaulted by youthful vandals. Damage has run to tens and even hundreds of thousands of dollars. These are not school-boy pranks. They are vicious gang assaults. Whether the youngsters call themselves Bishops or Rovers makes no difference. Their tactics would be the envy of their slum comrades. The school vandalism fever seems to have started on the Pacific Coast and spread east. It has virtually died out in the West. But it is in full flower in the East, particularly around New York.

A typical outbreak occurred at Maplewood, New Jersey, a fine community of middle-class families, proud of a low juvenile delinquency rate. A gang of boys broke into the Maplewood Junior High School and sacked it. They destroyed the principal's office, wrecked classrooms, carried kerosene and alcohol from the art department into the library, toppled books from the shelves, poured inflammables over them and set fire to the place. School authorities estimated the damage at $300,000. The school had to be closed for a week to make repairs.

Only after this outrageous attack did the community discover that there had been some signs that gang behavior was infecting the younger generation. There had been an increase, police said, in thefts of auto accessories and cars. Not long before the attack on the school a highway ice-cream parlor was wrecked one night after closing.

The Maplewood attack is outstanding only because of the extent of the damage. During a three-months period in the New York suburbs there were at least six similar outbreaks. Youngsters attacked a new $3,900,000 high school at West Islip, Long Island, smashing furniture, windows, throwing typewriters and tape recorders into the swimming pool, breaking up the principal's office and stealing the school station wagon. Another gang set four fires in the Uniondale, Long Island, High School, apparently in an effort to destroy truancy and grade records. A gang of seventeen youngsters attacked cars parked in the Valley Stream, Long Island, High School lot. They smashed windshields, slashed tires and tops. Two police cars parked on the lot were vandalized among the rest. A gang broke into the Memorial Library at Bellmore, Long Island, and set it afire, causing $65,000 damage. A gang broke into the new $3,500,000 high school in Passaic, New Jersey, spilling acid over the science laboratories, smashing bird specimens, breaking fish tanks, ripping down shelves and hurling India ink over walls and books.

Schools were not the only target of adolescent gang attacks. Teen-agers hurled smoke grenades into the swank Parkway Casino on the Bronx River Parkway while a high school dance was in progress. Fortunately, no one was injured. Another gang near Merrick, Long Island, killed a group of swans in a reservoir by hurling lighted sticks at them. Several youngsters from good families at Greenpoint, Long Island, took a car and spent a whole evening shooting out street lights and smashing school windows with air guns. A gang of ten youngsters broke into a beer warehouse at Sayville, Long Island, and set fire to it "to conceal their fingerprints" after making off with several cases of beer.

Youngsters of middle-class families have greater material resources than their young comrades in the street gangs. They usually employ a car in their escapades and manage to rove about the countryside to a startling degree. A group of three boys, fifteen, sixteen, seventeen, from good families in a nice suburb of San Antonio, Texas, ran away from their homes in mid-winter. They had a car and carted along with them more than three hundred pounds of canned goods and other supplies, apparently intending an extended stay in the wilderness. They drove to Florida, where one night they forced their way aboard a forty-foot yacht, terrorized a family of six to whom it belonged, and set sail for Cuba or Mexico—they weren't exactly sure which. In another day these boys might have wound up in the California gold rush or rounding the Horn in the forecastle of a four-masted sailing ship. But in this era they stole a cabin cruiser at gunpoint. The families said all of the boys were good youngsters. However, as is so often the case with the middle-class delinquent, there had been a trouble signal which was ignored. One of the boys had been arrested in a stolen car case, months before, it was revealed, but the case was not pressed.

There seems to be no limit to the sadistic ingenuity of teen-age delinquents. Possibly inspired by some comic strip adventure or the belated influence of a Pearl White serial, a bunch of boys in Norwalk, a suburb of Los Angeles, bound seven-year-old Michael Evans to the Santa Fe Railroad tracks. He was rescued by his father a minute or two before the express was due to whiz past.

It was in suburban Yonkers that some young gang boys got into an argument with four national guardsmen while their cars were waiting at a stoplight. When the light changed they swerved their car, forced the guards to the curb, leaped out and beat the militiamen badly with tire irons and jack handles. It was in suburban Belleville, New Jersey, that eighteen-year-old Nicholas Ucci lost an eye when he was dragged from the car in which he was riding and beaten by a rival gang in another car. And it was in West Hempstead, Long Island, that two cars laden with teen-agers were returning from a dance after midnight. The drivers began the dangerous game of veering at each other, turning at the last moment to avoid a collision. Finally the cars halted, nine youngsters, including two girls, piled out and a general melee ensued. Police halted the brawl after one boy was badly knifed.

These are just run-of-the-mill incidents in the better suburbs, for the most part, of the New York metropolitan area—the incidents which got on the record, which were not hushed up.

It is not only what is happening today which worries many social workers acquainted with suburban conditions. What alarms them most is what lies just ahead. In the years immediately after the war enormous numbers of jerry-built mass suburban developments sprang up on the flat sands of Long Island, the Jersey countryside, the vacant lands between Washington and Baltimore, the areas around Chicago and the endless vistas that surround Los Angeles. These cheaply built homes are largely populated by young working-class and lower-middle-class couples who started their families at about the same time, just after World War II. The birth rate in these communities is far higher than the national or the urban rates. The children of these families are just beginning to reach the age at which delinquency begins to manifest itself in more violent and destructive form. Thousands of these youngsters are moving into adolescence week-by-week and step-by-step together. Many of these communities are deficient in facilities for recreation for older children. Many of the families are not as strong or capable as they might be. Trouble, social workers fear, lies ahead in serious form.

This problem of the future is going to be much more like the delinquency problems of California than those of the teen-age gangs of Brooklyn. This new crop of mass-delinquents-to-be are going, for the most part, to be equipped with cars. They will be highway delinquents. Not street gangs. But the problem will be just as serious. Possibly more so.

The valid question arises as to what causes delinquency in these pleasant suburban areas. The children have all the conventional advantages. The homes are clean, neat, stuffed with consumer goods. The schools are good. There is ample room for kids to run and play. There are no dope pushers at the local candy stores to lure girls into prostitution. The families are not broken, for the most part. How does it happen that the kids go wrong?

The answer, I think, lies in a closer examination of the real conditions in many suburban homes. Behind an apparent façade of normality many a suburban home conceals just as broken a home as the Red Hook family from which the father has long since vanished.

As Professor Short found in his study of middle-class families in Washington State the key factor in delinquency is not the classic broken home from which one of the parents has departed but the "psychologically broken home." Divorce, he reports, is no infallible index to delinquency-breeding conditions. It is the children of unhappy homes, be they technically broken or not, who tend to go bad.

This fits the theory of Dr. Fred Brown of Mount Sinai Hospital that tensions in the life of the commuter often lead to instability in family relations, marital stress and delinquency on the part of the children. The sons, he says, are the principal victims of the situation, placed at an emotional distance from their father, often seeing little of him, reacting against domination of family life by the mother by extreme masculine attitudes, violence and even sadism.

In too many suburban homes the father sees little more of his children than does the alcoholic parent of the tenement family. In too many homes the mother is too busy with an eternal round of social activities to have any really warm relationship with her children. The end result is unhappiness in the midst of plenty. Children are as emotionally starved as those in the deprived areas of the slums.

Split-level delinquency in the quiet suburban communities is just as deadly a menace to the younger generation as are the festering conflicts of the housing projects and old slums.

8

the family

LAST summer there was no wilder, gayer girl in the crowd that tagged after the Cobras than Lucille. Bebop was her boy friend and she kept his piece, a nickel-plated revolver, hidden in a box under her bed. Lucille was fifteen last summer and it was the best summer of her life—something always doing with the Cobras, running around with Bebop, who was a Big Man in the gang, dancing at the center, especially with Bebop and letting him hold her very tight. Lucille's summer flew by on rainbow wings. There wasn't another place like Whitman Houses anywhere. Nor a better bunch of kids. That's what Lucille thought.

Lucille's sister, Joy, is two years younger. Her brother, Raymond, is a year older. All three children were born in Puerto Rico and came to New York ten years ago with their parents. Five years ago Mr. Gonzalez died. Mrs. Gonzalez has done her best to raise the family. City relief funds have been their main support for several years. They moved into Whitman Houses before Mr. Gonzalez died and it is the only real home the children have known.

The Gonzalezes don't think of themselves as unusual in any way. In their eyes there is little to distinguish them from their neighbors. They would be surprised to know that a special committee set up by New York's Mayor Robert F. Wagner classifies them as a "multi-problem" family. The "multi-problem" family is the newest catchword in the jargon of social studies. It is a new and convenient classification label. Every time one of these labels is invented, neat blue-covered reports are multilithed and distributed. There is an exchange of polite letters between the Mayor and the chairman of the study which invented the label. Then, the report is placed in the files with all the other studies. This gives the Mayor and other public officials a comfortable feeling. When criticism occurs they can always refer to the latest report, or to the forthcoming report, or, sometimes, even more fortuitously, to the "continuing study" now in progress. In the paperwork world where the bureaucrats live this is a most acceptable substitute for action.

The study of "multi-problem" families has revealed that there are twenty thousand families, constituting less than 1 per cent of the population of the city, which are the source of 75 per cent of all delinquency. This is what an earlier social studies cliché would call a "hard core." Of these twenty thousand families at least two thousand are numbered among the hundred thousand families who live in New York's low-rent housing projects.

One of the specks on the "dot map" which shows the geographic distribution of these families represents the Gonzalez family. Before last summer the Gonzalez family did not rate the distinction of a dot. Up to that time it was only a relief case. Outside of occasional truancy the youngsters had never been in trouble.

Then it began and, as is so often the case, once it started it happened fast. One evening in early fall Raymond was loafing around with a boy from the Cobras. The boy had a bottle and the two took a few drinks. They spotted a drunk weaving up the street, accosted him and ran off with his wallet. They were caught. Raymond had never done anything like this before. He was put on probation. Things might have worked out all right but the manager of Whitman Houses learned that Raymond had been in court and issued an eviction notice. Mrs. Gonzalez was beside herself. She began to lose her temper with her children, particularly with Lucille. Lucille was staying out later now with Bebop. Mrs. Gonzalez was worried. Her boy had gotten into trouble. She didn't want anything to happen to Lucille.

One Friday night there was a big dance at the center. All the teen-agers were there. Lucille was the life of the party— she and Poppy. Poppy's boy friend had a bottle of wine. He kept giving Lucille drinks. Finally she got sick and had to be helped home.

Mrs. Gonzalez put Lucille to bed without saying anything, but the next morning she started to lecture her daughter. She lost her head. She couldn't help it, what with the worry and the strain. Lucille sat white-lipped and pale as her mother ranted on. Suddenly, she leaped to her feet, rushed to the window, flung it open and jumped.

Lucille did not die in the four-story fall. Her back was broken. She was taken to Kings County Hospital and put into a plaster cast. It was weeks before the back began to heal. Lucille became more and more upset. Finally, she had to be taken to the psychiatric ward.

Lucille's trouble brought no reprieve from the housing project manager. Raymond quit school and began to work at a steady job, but the manager was adamant. Rules are rules. The Gonzalez family had to go. Somewhere Mrs. Gonzalez managed to find a moldering hovel which her relief check would pay for. Now the Gonzalez family has earned its dot. It is a full-fledged multi-problem family.

Mrs. Gonzalez' concern over her children and the love and affection which they felt for her proved inadequate to cope with the harsh pressure to which the family was subjected.

Over and over again this pattern is repeated. The family—where it exists—proves inadequate or is rendered inadequate to cope with life problems. And the children begin to go bad.

The New York Youth Board has plastered the city with a poster which simply says: When Family Life Stops, Delinquency Starts.

This homely truth has long been known but is often lost sight of in an eager search for more esoteric causation factors.

For several decades in the middle of the nineteenth century tribes of "Arab street boys" roamed the streets of New York. These were the shook-up kids of their generation, the children deposited in New York by the waves of immigration which inundated our shores. They were adolescents abandoned by their parents, apprentice boys, waifs left homeless by drunken parents, the forlorn offspring of lost or vanished fathers and mothers.

Charles Brace, a public-spirited citizen of his day, felt something should be done with these children. The only provision made by the city was the prison and workhouse. Mr. Brace sent carts around the city at night to pick up homeless youngsters. He set up a Newsboys Lodging Home where he fed and clothed them, gave them a little training with tools and prepared them to be sent out to farm families in Minnesota and Iowa. He dispatched agents to the West to find good homes for the boys and to see that they were not taken advantage of. It was Mr. Brace's old-fashioned belief that "the family is God's reformatory" and that the place for delinquent children who had lost their families was a home, a foster home if you like. On a pioneer farm there was always a place and a welcome for a boy. The soundness of Mr. Brace's theory was proved again and again as one-time street urchins grew up to be leading citizens of their communities.

When the family breaks down, due to nomadic movement of population, economic and technological pressure, war, or other stress, there is a patterned reaction by young people which transcends time and distance. It was probably identical in Caesar's rule and will be so a thousand years hence.

We think of modern America as a land where the wheel has replaced the hearthstone. It is true that the gasoline combustion society has developed a particularly rootless form. Millions of persons each year migrate from South to North, from East to West, from Midwest to East and from North to Southwest. These gigantic internal migrations have been common in each decade since the great depression set the Okies adrift on the highways to California in the early 1930's. World War II sent hundreds of thousands from the border states and the South into the factories of Detroit and Flint. Even more headed for the aircraft and shipyard plants of the Pacific Northwest and Southern California. Adolescent males in unprecedented numbers were uprooted from every corner, mobilized into the armed forces and dispersed like wheat in the wind to the earth's far ends.

The decade that followed World War II brought no end to the restless movement of the peoples. It intensified the tide from impoverished rural areas into Detroit, Los Angeles, the boom cities of Texas and New York.

While it would be difficult to demonstrate that a higher proportion of the American population was in motion in the mid-1950's than in the mid-1850's, when it sometimes seemed as though every family on the seaboard was headed for the Middle West and every family in the Middle West for further west, the two movements are of a more closely comparable order than may be generally supposed. Yet, there is a subtle difference between the two migrations. Today's movement is industrial, urban, often solitary. The family is unimportant. In 1858 the man of Shelby County, Ohio, who moved to Fillmore County, Minnesota, was a farmer, traveling with his wife and three children. They set up a life in Minnesota which differed little from that of Ohio. The same thing had happened a generation before in a movement to

Ohio from upstate New York. It was an agrarian movement and the family was the usual unit of migration. The family was an economic and social asset to be preserved and protected. If a man's wife died he promptly remarried. The same was true of the widow. Only a family could cope with a farm on the virgin prairie. This emphasis on the family unit probably held delinquency somewhat in check, but the frontier did not lack for problems associated with the antisocial adolescent.

Today we glamorize the frontier pistol kids and gunmen. We do not see the similarity of the gangs of trigger-happy youngsters who terrorized the Dakota Bad Lands and the gangs which rove the streets of Los Angeles or the Bronx. We forget that America has a deeply rooted tradition of violence. It is only a hundred years since statesmen ceased to carry sidearms into the halls of Congress. The vigilante tradition and mob rule are hard to distinguish from each other. Often it depended on who chased and who was chased. The James boys, the Younger brothers, Wyatt Earp, Hickok, and the rest of the Wild West names were, in a sense, the shook-up kids of their day.

As Pastor Oniki says, the "gang is just an example of mob psychology at work." This is hardly a new phenomenon on this side of the Atlantic.

In the frontier communities there was a premium upon toughness, physical force, readiness to use a gun and the ability to use it. The law west of Pecos was the law of the gun. There are neighborhoods in New York City and other big cities where the ruling mores have more in common with the frontier than with the conventions of middle-class society.

Take some of the tough areas of hard work near the New York docks. There is no economic problem. The men earn plenty of money. They preserve the saloon traditions of the Old West. The men drink at the neighborhood bars (while many a wife keeps a gin bottle concealed in a kitchen cabinet). The families are technically intact but spirtually fragmented.

In these areas adult gangsters are looked up to. A man makes his way up with his fists (or a knife and gun). Bookmakers and racketeers are respected. In this kind of neighborhood there is the same "idealization of personal violence" that John Dollard found in his classic sociological work, *Caste and Class in a Southern Town.* This dealt with a community not unlike those from which many have emigrated to New York, Chicago, Detroit and Dallas in recent years.

Mr. Dollard attributed the idealization to a breakdown in the formal machinery of law enforcement which compelled individuals to make and enforce their own laws.

"The inevitable result," he said, "is an atmosphere in which ability to defend one's right or to be the successful aggressor is highly prized. . . . It is more like the admiration felt on the frontier for the individual who is physically and morally competent to take care of himself."

There is often exactly this kind of breakdown in law enforcement where adolescents are concerned. The police are incapable of, or not interested in, protecting one adolescent from the violence of another unless property is endangered or adult lives are affected. The youngsters take the law into their own hands just as they did in the West. Often, they are encouraged by their parents. They may be coached never to give the other fellow an even break. As the father of an active gang member said: "The Youth Board is crazy. What are they trying to do? Kids always fight on the streets. You'll never change that."

In our persistent rationalization of reasons for human behavior we tend to color our views to suit the prejudices of the given moment. We think of the problems of the shook-up generation as unique to our time and our country. Yet, the pattern of youthful delinquency which is found on the streets of Harlem or the highways of East Texas has a counterpart not only in our own past but in many foreign countries, including the Soviet Union.

A famous Russian historical novel called *Grim River* opens with a description of a gang fight which might have occurred last night in Prospect Park. It involves teen-agers who battle it out in the central park of a Siberian city. The boys fight with "Finnish" knives, a long-bladed hunting knife not unlike those favored by certain East Harlem gangs. Such battles were common, the book makes clear, in the Russia of the last century.

They are still common today. I, myself, saw such a fight on a vacant lot just off the main street of Moscow. Two gangs slugged it out, hurling bricks and stones. One boy drew a knife, stabbed another in the back, and they all fled, leaving the wounded boy on the ground.

Few countries have had so much delinquency as the Soviet Union in its forty years of existence. This has stemmed from the enormous upheavals to which the population has been subjected, catastrophic uprootings of family units and family life. The Soviet state was born in such an upheaval, World War I with its loss of life and disruption of village and city. This merged into revolution, civil war, intervention, famine, starvation. By the time Bolshevik power had been established the country lay in ruins. Millions of lives had been lost. Hundreds of thousands of homeless, parentless, wandering children roamed the country. They formed gangs which preyed on the peasants and invaded the cities. They were called "wolf packs" or "wild children." They menaced life and security.

It was years before the situation was brought under control. A Ukrainian high school teacher named Makarenko did much work with these youngsters, using the same techniques now being employed with street gangs in our big cities. He won the confidence of the wild children by showing them friendship, by giving them a place to sleep, by helping them to get food and, sometimes, in the early days, by winking at their thefts when he had no food to give them.

Many of Makarenko's principles for dealing with upset Russian children, children without parents and without families, apply with equal soundness to our upset street gang youths with their background of broken and absent families. The Russians might teach us a lesson or two about teen-agers. They have had enough trouble with them. In the late 1920's Stalin launched the collectivization of agriculture. Hundreds of thousands of peasants were deported to Siberia. There was more famine. A whole new generation of upset, uprooted children was a by-product. The purge of the mid-1930's sent more adults to their graves or to Siberia and left new tens of thousands of orphaned, homeless youngsters. World War II smashed families right and left. Bands of wild children again appeared but by this time Russia had learned something about handling these problems. Many were put into institutions. Cavalry patrols took to the streets with shoot-on-sight orders against the worst of the street gangs. The situation was quickly brought under control.

If you visit Siberia today you will see thousands of youngsters shipped out from the streets of Moscow and other cities. They pour out of the factories at five in the afternoon, queuing up at the sidewalk vodka booths, fighting to hold a place in line in order to gulp down one hundred to two hundred grams of vodka and, sometimes, tumbling over onto the sidewalk to lie there drunk for hours, unnoticed, unregarded by pedestrians or police.

Antisocial conduct is not confined to working-class adolescents and uprooted peasant lads. The sons and daughters of the party secretaries, the cabinet ministers and the Army generals get involved as well. They are picked up by the police for stealing cars, selling their parents' property to get money for vodka sprees, gathering in country bungalows for wild parties with teen-age girls, getting arrested for drunkenness and disorderly conduct in cafés and restaurants. The delinquency of better-class Moscow youngsters more closely resembles that of their counterparts in Westchester than is sometimes supposed.

Russia also has a teen-age cult or sect called the *stilyagi* (the name means the stylish ones). They are like our zoot-suiters of a decade ago or the Teddy boys of England. They are in rebellion against banal Soviet society, the emptiness of their lives, the vapidness of Communist ideology. They run about in oddly dressed packs. They do not usually take part in gang combat although they have close relations with rougher youngsters who do. They engage sometimes in black-marketing and other conduct regarded as criminal or anti-social by the Soviet. They listen to rock 'n' roll over the foreign radio and bootleg their own recordings. Their musical taste resembles that of the Chimp and his fellow Rovers. They affect foreign dress—especially hand-painted neckties and wildly patterned American sports shirts. They wear drape-shape coats which reach to the knees, similar to those of the culturally backward diddley bops in Brooklyn. They wear their hair in a long bob like Johnny Weissmuller in the old Tarzan movies. They call their girl friends Jane as did Tarzan. They talk a peculiar idiom which mixes many English and French phrases with Russian. They call Gorky Street, Moscow's main thoroughfare, "Brodvai." They are first cousins of San Francisco's Undergrounds or the "Beat Generation." The relationship of the *stilyagi* to their counterparts in contemporary America is frequently the subject of bitter comment in the Soviet press.

This curious blend of the *jeunesse dorée* and the New York street boy has become an increasingly common feature of life behind the Iron Curtain.

The Hungarian revolution was set in motion by poets and patriots. But among its most vigorous recruits were the

Budapest street boys. If you talk extensively to the youngsters who participated in the events of October, 1956, you will quickly find that many who fought so valiantly against Soviet tanks were not politically conscious at all. But they were experienced, enthusiastic street fighters. In fact, they were exactly the kind of boys who rumble out in Astoria.

I was in Warsaw in October, 1957, at a time when there was continuous rioting on the streets for nearly a week. I saw the thousands of trench-coated youngsters in their snap-brim hats, taunting the police, provoking them into billy-swinging charges. As soon as the police charged the bully boys showered them with paving blocks and iron pipes. Then they ran down the street, dodged around a corner and gathered for a new foray. This demonstration had been started by university boys with a political cause. But it was quickly taken up by the thousands of bitter, idle Polish youngsters with no past and no perspective, flotsam of a society in a stage of transition. If these youngsters reached New York they could join the Cobras or the Rovers tomorrow. It would not take them long to learn "the sound."

In Western Europe there is no country where society seems more stable than the Netherlands. There, if anywhere, one would not expect to find problem teen-agers. But the Reverend Edward Rijnders, a young Presbyterian minister of Amsterdam, came to the United States in 1958 to study our methods of handling juvenile delinquency. And with good reason. His church has opened a youth center because of the serious situation on the Amsterdam streets.

"We have street gangs, just as you have in New York," Mr. Rijnders told me. "They fight gang against gang just like yours. They use the same dangerous weapons, revolvers, knives and any other kind of arms they can lay hands on."

The Amsterdam street gangs, he said, are made up of boys who are dull and backward in school. They are almost illiterate. Most are the children of working-class parents. Many are refugees from Indonesia.

"These boys have nothing in their lives," Mr. Rijnders said. "Before the war most working-class wives stayed home and looked after their families. Since the war factory pay has been so good that many of them work. Children are left alone when they come home from school. There is a bad housing problem, much overcrowding due to wartime destruction."

The Amsterdam street boys look for something to fight for. They join together to steal a car, rob a shop, get a girl whom all can share. If they have to fight another gang for the car, the shop or the girl, all the better. They fear—and hate—the police.

"The Communists have tried to enlist these boys," Mr. Rijnders said. "Amsterdam voted 30 per cent Communist in the last election. But the boys have no interest in politics. They have no interest in anything."

The Amsterdam teen-agers are nihilists. The only cause which arouses even faint enthusiasm is something which they can hate and fight.

I have no doubt that you could go around the world and in each society find youngsters whose families have disintegrated under pressure and who have banded together and formed themselves into hostile groups which defy the accepted order of society.

The picture is not a pleasant one. These upset youngsters of many lands share so many characteristics in common. And yet it is easy to generalize too broadly. Not all the boys in any adolescent antisocial group are lost. Many can be reclaimed by active social programs and there are some who will emerge by their own efforts little the worse for their experience. Where this happens the youngster almost invariably has the backing of a solid, healthy family. A good family can do more for the adolescent in trouble than all the social experts in the catalog.

What this means in real life can be seen in the case of Harold, a good-looking serious boy who is the vice president of an active street-fighting gang in one of the Brooklyn housing projects. The gang boys look to Harold with confidence and respect, but he is a boy who has never "gone down," who has never engaged in bopping at all. It always happens that on the night the club goes out to fight he is made to stay home; or he is ill; or he is spending a week's vacation with his aunt away from New York. Yet, he does not lose status with his comrades.

Harold stands in the middle of the violence but is not of it. I think the same would be true if Harold lived in the suburbs of Warsaw or in the slums of Amsterdam. He does well in his studies. He does not go to school in Brooklyn. He picked a Manhattan high school deliberately, "because I knew what would happen if I went to school with all the other guys."

You understand Harold better after you talk to his father, an even-tempered sign painter who enjoys his four children and spends a lot of time with them. His wife is pleasant and comfortable. They live in one of the worst housing projects in the city, but in their apartment you see a good TV set, a bookcase with an encyclopedia and two shelves of books. Harold's father does not enforce his will with his fists. He talks things over with his son. Harold belongs to the gang because that is the pattern in the project, but his family gives him strength to keep from being pushed into extreme antisocial conduct. Because Harold's family is a vigorous, effective unit of society he stands a good chance of emerging unscathed from the dangerous world in which he lives. In the long run this is what counts in the preservation of adolescents.

Most of the gang youngsters wherever they may be are

hardly so fortunate. Even if by dint of their own efforts they manage to pull themselves out they cannot be sure that some fateful mischance will not strike them down.

This is what worries Stoney, a small man of twenty-three years who used to be a leading fighter in the Chaplains of Brooklyn. Stoney was married last year. He has a job. He has given up the gang. He is doing his best to make a new "cool" life. But it is not easy.

The other night, as he was coming home from a party with his wife, he was attacked by three juvenile gang members.

"It's the little ones who are dangerous, man," he says. "They don't care what they do. If you don't want them to hurt you, you have to hurt them. But that is dangerous, man. You might kill them. That would be the chair for you.

"We older fellows—we've got to go cool. Gotta cool it now, man. But those little ones coming up. They're the real problem. Something's got to be done about them, or I don't know where we'll be at."

Stoney agrees with Doc, the old dentist in *West Side Story,* who tells the teen-age Jets that "you kids are making this a lousy world." But he also agrees with the kids who retorted: "But that's the way we found it."

To which the *stilyagi* of Moscow, the youthful drunkards of Siberia, the teen-age fighters of Budapest, the sullen rioters of Warsaw, the nihilists of Amsterdam, and all the other shook-up youngsters around the world would say, Amen.

9

the schools and the gang

A LITTLE past mid-morning on Tuesday, January 28, 1958, George Goldfarb, a man of medium height, fifty-five years old, wearing glasses with silvered rims and carrying an umbrella, entered a six-story building at 201 Eastern Parkway, Brooklyn. Mr. Goldfarb lived in this apartment house, which is located in an average middle-class residential section. On Tuesday morning, however, he did not go to the flat where his wife was doing her household chores. Instead, he entered the self-service elevator and pushed the button for the sixth floor. At the sixth floor he emerged from the elevator, walked down the corridor to the steel door giving access to the roof, opened it and went out on the asphalt surface.

Mr. Goldfarb walked to the edge of the roof. He carefully put down the black silk umbrella. There had been a drizzle earlier in the morning but it was now beginning to clear. He took one step to the narrow parapet and leaped over.

A few minutes later, at precisely ten minutes before noon, the superintendent of the apartment house discovered Mr. Goldfarb's body in the rear courtyard where he had fallen. A few feet away were his broken glasses. The medical examiner said that death had been instantaneous.

Mr. Goldfarb, a rather quiet, reserved man, very conscientious, very painstaking—indeed, regarded by his colleagues as almost too concerned about his duties—was the principal of John Marshall Junior High School in Brooklyn. He had served in the New York City public schools for over thirty-three years, ever since his graduation from college, and had been principal of John Marshall High for four years. He had a grown-up son living in San Francisco. His neighbors described him as an unassuming but dignified man. They liked him and had always gotten on well with him.

Mr. Goldfarb was not a schoolman of outstanding attainment. He was, however, a good example of the hard-working, serious individuals in New York and throughout the country who devote themselves to preparing our children to face the problems of the contemporary world. Mr. Goldfarb did not earn as much money as the manager of a moderate-volume supermarket. His hours were long, his responsibilities demanding and his prospects for advancement limited. But he enjoyed his work and it was the career he had chosen for himself.

On the morning of his death Mr. Goldfarb had reported to his school as usual, shortly before 8 A.M. He conferred with his two assistant principals and the personnel of his office. At nine o'clock he turned on the office radio to listen to the morning broadcast of directives from Public School Head quarters at 110 Livingston Street, Brooklyn. At about 9:30 he left his office. His secretary recalled later that she had to remind him to take his umbrella. He told the assistant principals that he had to appear at 10 A.M. before a special grand jury which had been empaneled by Judge Samuel Leibowitz of Kings County Court to investigate violence in the Brooklyn schools.

Mr. Goldfarb had testified twice already before the grand jury. After his suicide the charge was made that he had been hounded to death by brutal cross-examination. It is beyond question that the jury took a tough line with witnesses in the school inquiry and, no doubt, with Mr. Goldfarb. He had been called because of several incidents of violence at John Marshall school. A careful examination of these incidents, after Mr. Goldfarb's suicide, indicated that their significance had been exaggerated in the heated atmosphere of the grand jury inquiry. Violence had occurred at John Marshall but neither on the scale nor to the degree which the grand jury's action might suggest. The fact is that John Marshall was not then and never had been a particular trouble center. But once the grand jury's spotlight centered there everything that happened was magnified out of proportion.

Exactly what led Mr. Goldfarb to take his life cannot be said with certainty. He had been browbeaten, insulted and possibly threatened before the grand jury. It was even charged that the jury told Mr. Goldfarb that it was going to "get" him. Yet, when he left his school office at 9:30, supposedly headed for the Kings County courthouse, Mr. Goldfarb said that there was "nothing to worry about," that this was just a routine appearance. Obviously Mr. Goldfarb was much more worried and concerned than he permitted his associates or even his wife to imagine.

After the Goldfarb tragedy two tendencies emerged in public discussion of the situation in the New York schools. One was to blame the grand jury for persecuting the school system and its directors and, thus, inferentially to shift discussion away from the question of what had caused the violence in the schools and the degree, if any, to which school authorities were to blame for the situation. The other was to heap up so many reports of incidents and outrages in the schools that the suicide of Mr. Goldfarb became almost lost in the hourly bulletins of stabbings, killings, assaults, and rapes.

Both these viewpoints completely overlooked the main question, which is, what is the cause of adolescent violence and what can be done by the schools to reduce this violence and to save the talents, skills and abilities of the shook-up generation for the benefit of the nation as well as themselves.

Regardless of the overt role played in Mr. Goldfarb's death by the grand jury inquiry there can be no question but that this mild, goodhearted man's life was forfeit because of the impact of the shook-up generation on the public education system. He was a victim of the street gangs of New York and of the society which permits their growth and spread just as surely as if he had been stabbed with a switchblade, shot by a zip gun or run down by the automobile of a teen-age motor murderer.

There has been such a wave of headlines about teen-age youth and the New York schools since Mr. Goldfarb's death that the real facts have almost been buried under the printer's ink. The impression has spread throughout the country that the New York public schools are engulfed by a reign of terror. Frightened parents make plans to move from Manhattan to the suburbs. Alarmed suburban communities fear lest the plague of outrages spread to their peaceful schools. Editorialists thunder. The inevitable demands for "drastic action" arise. The Board of Education gets panic-stricken. Teachers threaten to resign. Southerners eagerly devour reports that Negro and Puerto Rican teen-age mobs rule the roost in the New York schools. New York is worse than Little Rock, they say.

It is well to get the matter into perspective. Scare headlines are not necessarily the best barometer. There are more than 900,000 youngsters in the New York City public schools. In any group of 900,000 children, whatever their geographic or cultural origin, at least one case of violent misbehavior might be anticipated on any given day. This is an extreme low estimate. Misbehavior is contagious. If you have one case you are apt to have two. It only takes one upset child to cause more trouble than a dozen adults can handle comfortably. Ask any parent. Or any teacher.

So the fact that nearly every day somewhere in New York a schoolboy scuffles with a teacher, injures another boy in a fight with deadly weapons or is discovered "raping" a girl in a janitor's closet cannot, in the statistical sense, be regarded as extraordinary. This is merely adolescence performing according to the law of averages. If anything, the over-all ratio of violence to the total school population seems low. At a guess there are areas of the United States where the incidence of misbehavior in the schools runs higher.

Because of the overemphasis which has lately been placed on the damaged segment of our adolescent generation, the shook-up fraction, it will do no harm to state that 99 per cent of New York City school pupils, like 99 per cent of the pupils of schools all over America, are good boys and girls, their conduct unaffected by gang mores. They study their lessons and want to do well. Perhaps they do not apply themselves as hard to their lessons as we would wish. Perhaps they spend more time listening to the juke and rock 'n' roll than we think is right. But there is no simple equation between a taste for Elvis Presley and a taste for switchblades. This goes for children of all races, creeds, colors, sizes, shapes and varieties.

And to give the street gangs their due, much of the time these youngsters are engaged in nothing more harmful than time wasting and boredom. Gangs are shifting and fluid groups. A youngster may indulge in violent antisocial conduct on the street. When he enters the school he often adopts the coloration of the group he is in. Most gang boys are dull or backward in school but they are not necessarily bad actors.

Nevertheless when you have large numbers of these youngsters in a school, when they have, like Pavlov's dogs, been subjected to so many bewildering shocks by life that their reaction patterns become erratic, unpredictable and frequently dangerous to themselves and others, you introduce a very uncertain factor into the classroom. Trouble may break out at any time—and for no reason which even an alert teacher necessarily observes. It may have a source far away from the study section. Knowledge that she is conducting her lessons in a situation which may suddenly explode can unnerve a teacher—to the point that she herself triggers the outburst by revealing a lack of certainty of control.

But, again, the equation gang-equals-trouble does not always hold true. There are schools attended by conflicting gang groups which themselves maintain internal order by enforcing a "cool" on school territory. I have visited such schools. They are as quiet and orderly as many of the Moscow schools with their currently much vaunted discipline.

On the other hand a Brooklyn school principal told me of a school in which two gangs, the Bishops and the Stonekillers, fought it out for two years for control of the school. The battling went on until the Bishops won out. The school was not a pleasant one during this conflict. Now the school is quiet, an uneasy truce is enforced, not by the authority of the principal but by the authority of a sixteen-year-old street club president.

The suggestion is often advanced by those who have not examined the schools at first hand that race conflict lies behind much of the violence. I do not know of a single New York school official who has seen evidence to support this idea. The Reverend Milton A. Galamison of the National Association for the Advancement of Colored People told me that the Association had not heard of a single instance of tension or racial feeling in the New York schools. "We would know," he said, "because the NAACP would be called in immediately and no such call has been received."

As one school principal told me: "We have imported a lot of social problems from Puerto Rico, South Carolina, and other points where these children originate. We are paying for the lack of cultural progress and social backwardness of those areas. But one thing has not been imported—racial differences."

An impression born of the headlined violence is that New York classrooms are so intimidated by the shook-up youngsters that ordinary pupils cannot study and teachers cannot teach. The schools are envisaged as besieged fortresses, windows barred with iron, doors double-bolted against assault from without, playgrounds surrounded by barbed wire, guards at the entrance doors, patrols of police inside and gang boys shooting it out with Berettas, smuggled into the schools in lunchboxes.

This is a myth.

So is the idea that the trouble in the schools and, indeed, much of the difficulty with our adolescents was generated by the schools themselves and the teachers—specifically by so-called progressive or permissive systems of education. Advocates of this view feel that because children are "coddled," because the birch rod has been taken out of the teacher's hand, because learning has been made more pleasant, the adolescent generation has gone to wrack and ruin, formed into gangs and taken to carrying out bloody rumbles.

I think that Dr. Lawrence Feigenbaum, a veteran New York schoolman and the assistant principal of a Brooklyn school with a rapidly increasing enrollment of Puerto Ricans, was much closer to reality when he told me:

"The kids reflect the adults and the world they live in. People have less to hold on to today. What have they got to believe in? We live in an era of violence and speed. The emphasis is on material things."

His views are shared by his colleague, Irving Levin, principal of the school.

"We try to make them act the way we don't," Mr. Levin said. "We try to teach them to be polite, to be generous, to believe in the sacredness of human life, to respect the rights of others. But the kids have eyes. They look around. They see that ultimately individuals and nations use force to solve their problems. They think that we are hypocrites because we tell them about the old-fashioned virtues. On the one hand we urge them to save money. On the other we urge them to spend it all on the installment plan. We do not practice the virtues which we preach in private life, community life or in foreign relations."

What has been lost sight of in the hysteria over the violence in the schools is the fact that for all their shortcomings the schools are the most positive factor in the lives of the problem children.

"The youngsters don't realize it," Mr. Levin said. "Some teachers don't realize it. But, by and large, the kids behave better in school than anywhere else—better than they do at home and better than they do on the street. It is not easy for many of them. They are not mature enough for education. Later they realize this. There are not many kids who really don't want an education."

Dr. Robert M. MacIver, director of the New York City Juvenile Evaluation Project, shares this view. He has devoted years of study to the delinquency problem.

"The school is the most stable social institution which the children encounter," he said. "It is the only structural organization which many of them know. The only one which can help them.

"They come from broken families. The church stands aside. The courts and the police are regarded as the enemy. The school is often the only helping hand. When the time for police intervention has come it is already too late."

If the members of the shook-up generation come closer to meeting the norms of social behavior in the schools than anywhere else, what actually lies behind the outbreaks of violence that do occur in the classroom? Is this really school trouble or it is trouble which is imported from the family or the community outside school? What is the actual role of the school in these situations?

I have examined the background of enough actual outbreaks to satisfy myself that in many cases the fact that they happened in the school was clearly accidental.

Let us look at a typical example. The newspapers reported that one teen-ager shot another at Manual Training High School in Brooklyn.

To find out why the boy was shot and how the weapon got to school it is necessary to go back ten days earlier to a chain of events involving our old friends the Cobras and the Silver Arrows, on the one hand, and the Rovers and the Apaches, on the other.

One Friday night when I happened to be visiting their turf a party of about twenty Cobras and Arrows boarded a subway in a gay and venturesome mood. They were very mysterious about their destination but it later turned out that they had heard that another club was giving a party to which the Cobras wouldn't "dare" show up. This was a challenge the Cobras would not let pass.

"You should be there when they knock on that door," a friend told me. "They'll explode into that apartment like John Dillinger. Just a look from anyone will start trouble. If someone sounds them that joint will be a wreck in the morning."

However, this expedition came to nothing. They never found the party. Perhaps there wasn't any. Maybe it was the wrong night. Or the wrong address. Or a girl starting trouble.

This set the stage for Saturday night. On Saturday night the Cobras and Arrows were invited to a "house party" by an Arrow member who lived not in Whitman Houses but just outside on the turf of the Rovers. A "cool" was in force so that, technically, there was no reason for not going. On the other hand the incursion of a large alien group is always resented. But after the fiasco of the night before the Arrows and Cobras felt belligerent. If the Rovers didn't like it they could shove it.

The party had just gotten going nicely, the youngsters were "fishing" to the music of a record player, several bottles of wine had been passed around, when a rock smashed through a window. The boys plunged to the street and a wild melee followed. By some accident no one got worse than a black eye. Neither side would take this lying down. On Sunday the forces massed at the local movie matinee, forty to fifty boys on each side, ready for trouble. But special details of police were on hand and no fighting ensued.

That night, street club workers got the boys to agree that no serious issues were involved and a cool was called. Things were quiet for a couple of nights. Then a group of Cobras and Arrows took a gun into Rover territory and fired a volley of shots. This was a warning and a challenge.

The next night the Rovers caught an Arrow and beat him up.

The trouble was on again. Friday night, traditional bopping night, was coming up. This is the night street club workers pray for rain. This Friday proved no exception to the tradition. A girl friend of one Rover claimed an Arrow had slapped her. The Rovers invaded Whitman Houses to avenge the insult but, fortunately, found no Arrows around. Finally a street club worker managed to establish that all the Arrows had been in the Community Center at the time of the alleged incident. But then a new rumor spread. This was that two Puerto Rican boys had been attacked by the Apaches, allies of the Rovers.

This was even more s   conflict was spreading.

Saturday was a tense a
workers managed to arrange

leader of the Arrows, and the Apaches. As is often the case
the facts were not what had been supposed. The boys involved in the fight with the Apaches were not local residents. They belonged to the Fort Greene Mau Maus. They
had not been japped in the mistaken belief that they were
Arrows. They themselves had started the fight.

Once again a cool was decreed.

By this time there had been ten days of tension. All the
youngsters were on guard against ambush and attack. And
this is where Manual Training School became involved.
Many Rovers go there. As a defensive precaution they had
been carrying a pistol to school. They were afraid that the
weapon would be found so they kept passing it from one
boy to another. No one boy kept it long. In one of these
transfers from boy to boy a youngster inexperienced in
firearms accidentally discharged the pistol, wounding his
classmate. A Police Department Youth Squad happened to
be at the school at the time. They arrested the boy, found
that the weapon had passed through the hands of at least
ten others, got their names, and hauled them all in. The
blow crippled the fighting strength of the Rovers.

The school was nothing but an accidental stage setting
for this outbreak of violence.

Often, of course, the involvement is more direct. The
shook-up youngster is a difficult boy. He is not easy to
handle. He gives trouble to experienced teachers and not
all teachers are experienced. Not all can recognize abnormal
adolescent behavior. Not all know what to do when they
do witness it. Teachers are human. They get tired. They
have their own worries. They make mistakes.

Nothing could have ███████████ by Manual Training High
to avoid the sh██████████ ort of searching each boy
as he arriv█████████████ure which is followed at
some s████████████████the most disturbed young-
███████████████████ol and its teachers may be

directly concerned. Such cases merit serious scrutiny in an effort to see how they might have been avoided.

One of these cases which I looked into involved Public School 27 in the Red Hook section of Brooklyn. There is much gang activity and street fighting in this neighborhood and the school is on the "difficult" list of the Board of Education.

The incident at P.S. 27 drew even bigger headlines than the one at Manual Training High. It involved a fourteen-year-old boy who was described as "going for" a teacher with the jagged end of a broken bottle. It sounded like something out of *Blackboard Jungle*. Anyone reading the story would wonder how any teacher could be persuaded to stay in the New York school system. I knew that this kind of publicity was giving the Board of Education increasing difficulty in recruiting teachers and decided to see what lay behind it—whether the school, the individuals, the community, or the family was primarily at fault.

The youngster, I discovered, was a boy named Thompson and he was a member of one of the street clubs with which I had become acquainted. The attack had occurred some weeks previously but he was still being held in Youth House while his case awaited disposition. The wheels of the law do not turn with great rapidity where these youngsters are concerned.

Thompson, I found, was a boy who was well liked in the local community house and never had given any trouble there. One of the street club workers knew him and had been trying to help him. He said the boy's home was not a bad one, that he was a good boxer and hoped to become a prize fighter.

The worker went down to visit Thompson at Youth House. He found him lonesome. His father had only been to see him once and his mother a couple of times.

"I missed you," Thompson told the worker.

"I told him he was going to be missing me for quite a while," the worker said. "I told him he was absolutely out of line and had no right to do what he did."

After talking to Thompson's friends at the community center I visited P.S. 27 and looked up Isaac O. Gimprich, the principal. Mr. Gimprich is a serious educator who has spent many years of his career in difficult schools. He has been principal of P.S. 27 for six years. For a long time he acted as principal of a Hebrew school after his public school day was done. But he has given that up because of the strain.

Mr. Gimprich has his problems at P.S. 27. Half the pupils are Negro, 20 per cent of them are Puerto Rican and the rest are of Italian, Irish, Norwegian and Jewish origin. It is a big school on a two-shift schedule. With all his responsibilities it would not have been surprising if Mr. Gimprich had not known Thompson. But this was not the case at all.

"Thompson is a boy whom I was trying to help," Mr. Gimprich said with a nervous gesture of his shoulders. "He had been held over and spent two years in seventh grade. This year he was in eighth but he was having difficulty. He came into my office one day and I asked him what the trouble was. He said the book was too hard. He couldn't read it. I gave him an easier book and told him to sit down and see if he didn't find it easier."

Thompson responded very well. He took the book, and began to read it with interest.

"I had to leave my office," Mr. Gimprich said. "I told him, 'You look after my office while I'm gone. See that everything is O.K.'"

Thompson liked that. Mr. Gimprich asked the boy if he would brush the snow off his Plymouth, which was parked outside. Thompson did the chore and said he would be glad to clean the inside of the car as well.

"I gave him the car keys," Mr. Gimprich said. "He did it twice for me, very, very nicely. I trusted him."

Mr. Gimprich recognized perfectly well that Thompson was a problem boy but he also saw that he was a youngster with positive qualities who could be worked with and who reacted well to help.

Yet, one afternoon when several classes were in the school gym, an order was given to the children to sit down. Thompson did not sit down. The instructor tried to force Thompson to sit. Thompson swung at the teacher, catching him in the lip and causing it to bleed. The teacher ordered the boy into a small office off the gym and closed the door behind him.

Thompson was frightened. He thought the teacher was going to give him a beating. He saw an empty Coke bottle on the windowsill, grabbed it, knocked off its head and turned to face the teacher. The teacher slung a chair at the boy and called for reinforcements. The boy was overpowered and turned over to the police.

Why did it happen? Thompson doesn't know. "I just lost control," he told the street club worker. One of Thompson's companions said, "When you lose control you don't know what you are doing. You do anything."

I met Thompson a little later after he had been up in Children's Court and released on probation. He is a soft-speaking youngster with a slow, warm smile. He weighs about 115 pounds, is light on his feet and speaks with a Georgia drawl.

He was transferred to another school which he did not like as well as P.S. 27 but was determined to stay out of trouble. He told me about the four fights he had had so far and his plans for going back into training. He hoped to get a job during the summer vacation.

"A better one than last summer, I hope," he said. "Last summer I worked on the bleach truck. You carry two five-gallon cans. You go up and down all the time. One in each hand. 'Anybody want any bleach? Nice fresh bleach!' Man, that's hard work even for fourteen dollars a week."

Mr. Gimprich made no secret over his concern about the Thompson incident. The boy should not have acted as he did. But the principal does not believe the school was blameless.

"We should have been able to prevent it," he said. "But, perhaps, we all learned something from it."

The Thompson case seems to underline the difficulty of helping disturbed youngsters without running the risk of behavior explosions. But it also underlines the efforts which are made in even the difficult schools, the ones we imagine to be "blackboard jungles," to try to work with youngsters on a human, affectionate basis.

This kind of work is at the opposite pole from the "shock action" ordered by New York's School Superintendent, Dr. William Jansen, during the hysteria which followed Mr. Goldfarb's suicide. More than nine hundred difficult and "dangerous" youngsters were suspended from the school system under drastic orders issued by the Superintendent.

It might be natural to suppose that a difficult school like P.S. 27 with its high quota of shook-up pupils would have many suspensions. Indeed, it surprised me a little that Thompson had not been suspended.

But Mr. Gimprich's attitude was much more humane, much more in the great tradition of American education than the "kick 'em out" philosophy epitomized by the suspension edict.

Mr. Gimprich asked his teachers how many youngsters should be suspended. They gave him six names. Instead of suspending these youngsters he decided to see if they could not be rehabilitated by giving them special teaching assistance and studying their problems individually.

His first discovery was that in each instance the youngsters were at least two years retarded in reading. This finding was in accord with what I heard from every individual who had anything to do with delinquent or problem children. Almost without exception these children are far behind the average levels in reading.

In the special schools which New York has set up to take care of youngsters who are behavior problems, test after test shows the correlation of low reading ability and antisocial conduct. The conclusion of educators is that nonreading is an early symptom of an antagonistic and aggressive reaction by the child against authority or against discipline and the accepted way of doing things. Once the reading handicap begins to emerge and the child falls further and further behind, a spiral process is set up in which inability to read increases the child's disturbance and the disturbance increases the stubbornness of the block against learning.

Finally, the combination cripples the child as a participant in the normal outlets of his own society. School becomes a torment and an endless source of wounds to pride and ego.

"These youngsters do not respect themselves," Mr. Gimprich said. "They cause trouble. They try to gain attention by being nuisances."

Mr. Gimprich assigned special remedial reading teachers to each pupil. He gave them extra assistance in arithmetic as well. He brought in their parents for consultation.

"It's too soon to say," he said. "But I'm hopeful that we will be able to salvage these six children instead of turning them loose to the school of the streets."

A guidance specialist in one of the New York schools for problem children said of the reading problem:

"Let's remember that many of our children come from homes where there is a very low reading level. There are few books in the home. Little interest in reading. This goes for many better homes as well as those of deprived families. They don't use libraries. They look at picture books and picture papers. Many youngsters are not ready mentally to start their reading lessons. They have not been in school consistently. They have been moved around. They get off to a bad start. It gets worse as it goes on. Blocks develop. They do badly in school and this builds up hostility to school—and to reading. This is the biggest single problem with delinquent youngsters."

It is hard for many of us to imagine how narrow the world must be for youngsters who cannot read well enough to study elementary lessons let alone literature, history, poetry or philosophy. Yet hundreds of thousands of teen-agers are growing toward adulthood with minds which are crippled by their inability to unlock the key of the printed page.

Perhaps if the Brooklyn grand jury had directed its questioning of Mr. Goldfarb to such matters as how the youngsters at John Marshall High are being taught to read the glories of Shakespeare, Goethe and Tolstoy; what steps are being taken to insure that every backward child is being given a chance to catch up with his fellows; what aids the community could give the school in accomplishing these vital tasks, the principal would be alive today and pursuing his duties with unaccustomed vigor and enthusiasm.

Indeed, it is not too late for this lesson to be taken to heart. Nor is it one which need be confined to New York. Delinquency exists in every community of America. Ignorance is its handmaiden. The simple device of teaching our children to read with efficiency and pleasure would not eliminate all the troubles. But it would give street society a real competitor.

10

the schools—a positive approach

OUR schools have been blamed lately for most of the ills of the day. They are called breeding places for juvenile delinquency. They are attacked from both flanks in the integration controversy. They are indicted because we are falling behind Russia in the space age.

I have visited a good many schools, largely in New York, talked to a great many of the youngsters who attend them, to the teachers, to the principals and to specialists in many fields of education.

No one can come away from even a modest survey without perceiving that the educational system has faults. That poor schools contribute to delinquency is demonstrable. That delinquency makes for poor education is obvious. That integration complicates many educational matters is beyond question. And there is no doubt that recent Soviet technological achievements compel us to undertake the most critical re-examination of the educational process.

May it be that all these questions are part of a single larger problem? I think this possibility merits examination. After all there is more than one sociologist who believes high rates of delinquency among Negroes and other minorities arise from national discrimination. And is it not likely that those factors which prevent us from resolving the minority problem are also responsible for our failure to maintain our enormous technological advantage over the Soviet Union? The essence of both of these problems is simply one of our basic attitude toward people and the utilization of human resources.

To what extent can we blame the schools for the situation in which we find ourselves?

There are some who put the responsibility upon educational administrators, the career products of the teachers' schools and colleges, the men who run so many of the larger educational systems, the professional schoolmen. They are indicted for excessive concentration on method and routine, for pettifoggery and red tape. For example, in New York City sharp criticism has been directed toward the Board of Education and, particularly, the recent Superintendent, Dr. William E. Jansen. One salty-tongued Brooklyn educator refers to the Board of Education offices at 110 Livingston Street as "the Kremlin." Another man who has fought long and hard for improvement of the New York schools said in a mood of deep depression:

"The Board of Education does not know and does not care whether conditions improve in the schools. All it really is interested in is its own skin."

He believes that education too often has become a fraud on the taxpayer's dollar. He pays and pays. Not for teaching, not for education—for bureaucracy.

"A whole miasma of jargon has been invented to explain why children can't learn and don't learn," he said. "Instead of insisting on performance by the teachers and by the students the bureaucrats fall back on catchwords which seem to justify failure. They throw up a smoke screen of technical language. It is all meaningless. The taxpayer finally gives up in disgust."

Or as Professor Kenneth Clark of City College put it:

"The real problem is hypocritical bureaucracy, protective of its kingdom, ready to use bullying, blackmailing or any other weapon to maintain the status quo. The real jungle is in the office of the bureaucrats, not on the streets to which we consign the youngsters."

While these words are directed specifically to the New York situation they apply with equal force to many other school systems. Mediocrity has too long been enthroned in too many places. This may be why I found in talking with educators an almost universal tendency to equate change, any change, with progress and to prefer the new to the old merely because it is new. Of course, this mirrors the mores of our society. We Americans live by the cult of the new and the cult of the material. So much has this become the fabric of our existence that it is rare, indeed, to find a schoolman who even recognizes these national cults, let alone the contribution which they make to the problems which we call on the schools to solve—the shook-up generation, competition with Russia, race relations.

It is not often in these times that a schoolman's mind inclines to philosophical thought and least of all to any questioning of the well-established postulates of our society. Yet, surely it is in our value system that the germ of the trouble lies hidden.

"We tend to forget our relationship with our fellows and are on the path toward inhumanity," Dr. Albert Schweitzer has written. "Increasingly, there is lost the consciousness that every man is an object of concern for us just because he is a man, civilization and morals are shaken and the advance to fully developed inhumanity is only a question of time.

"In the education and the school books of today the duty of humanity is relegated to an obscure corner. . . . It has not always been so."

The path toward inhumanity . . . these words strike with special force when you ask a teacher about sources of juvenile delinquency and he talks about the need for staff parking lots or changes in the pension plan.

It is a rare school principal who does not begin to discuss his problems in terms of physical plant—material things. He equates new buildings with progress, with better teaching, a better school, improved education. It seems never to occur to him that there is no correlation between tile brick and knowledge. Perhaps the new building costs less to keep up but the accountants who figure these things out also bow to the cult of the new. It may be that the cost of borrowing money to build the new school would more than pay the extra custodial fees on the old.

It must be new and it must be different. This is the law of modern education. Yet, it is hard to see how children have changed in seventy-five years. Or teachers, either. Why change the classrooms? Have children's behinds really changed so much that they require the pressed-wood shapes of "posture" chairs? There are obvious advantages to using a slate which can be erased, again and again. Pastel chalk and colored blackboards are new. Are they really *better?* Do children in an old room with tall windows and a high ceiling really get less light and air than children in a new room with low ceilings, small windows and fluorescent lighting?

Must the good always be the new? Haven't the schools, the principals and the school boards fallen victim to the same cheap sales psychology which fleeces the Puerto Rican families; in chasing the rainbow of this year's model aren't educators neglecting the true and the basic; aren't they contributing to the shaking of "civilization and morals" which concerns Dr. Schweitzer? Change for the sake of change is the rule. The virtue of permanence and unchanging foundations is lost. Small wonder that the younger generation finds it difficult to pick a straight path through a world of such fleeting values.

I have met few principals who do not complain if their

school is an old four- or five-story walk-up. But it is doubtful if youngsters have lost the energy they possessed half a century ago. It is more than doubtful that walking up and down stairs does them anything but good. The same may be said for the teachers. The fad today is to have everything on one floor like a supermarket. What connection this has with education is hard to see. What bothers the principals in the old schools is Thorstein Veblen's theory of ostentatious emulation. The fancy new schools being built in the fancy new suburbs are all one-story with movable walls, movable desks, movable seats. The old school is "obsolete." This makes the principal feel obsolete.

The confusion of newness with goodness runs all through the schools. Nowhere does it reach such a height as in the textbook business. I use the word "business" out of a sense of delicacy. There are stronger and more accurate words. Each year a torrent of multi-hued texts pours from the presses of the commercial manufacturers. These gentlemen operate on the General Motors theory. Each year a new model. Add tail fins. Add more chrome. Zip! Last year's geography is out of date. Sell the suckers a new one.

Small wonder that school libraries suffer. Who can afford to buy the classics and keep up with the contemporary output as well? Children grow up, generation after generation, unread and untaught in things worth while. There is no profit margin in Gibbons and Prescott. No room for the old if we are to keep the textbook industry profitable and productive. Cooper and Hawthorne? Dickens and Thackeray? Those are *last* century's authors. This is a new era. We must keep up with the times. Be up to date. Get the new plastic-covered, simplified, multi-national text with the 1,001 illustrations (produced by a collaboration of three authorities and making last year's text absolutely outdated), complete with teacher's guide, classroom aids, suggested examinations and predigested grading capsules. Absolutely tasteless. Absolutely harmless.

All the vulgar, facile tricks of the cheap magazine picture press are eagerly (if badly) imitated by the textbook producers. In some schools the weekly picture journals are even foisted on the children as "current literature"! No one in the community, except possibly Admiral Rickover, challenges these concepts. None of the principals do. No one ever asks by what right pulp paper processors have taken over the function of deciding what texts the children should use. The school administrators accept the commercial product just as they accept the criteria of newness because this is the way women's hats, new furniture and automobiles are sold. If it is good enough for Seventh Avenue, Grand Rapids and Detroit, it's good enough for the Board of Education.

Not that I believe we can hold the bureaucratic administrators at fault for these attitudes. They are not prime movers. They are pawns of the system.

In the field of education, after all, we get just what we deserve and just what we pay for. If we have been content for many years to short-change the schools in order to keep down tax rates; if we let the professionals run the schools in their own way (except for specific problems involving Johnny); if we do nothing to halt the vigorous, child-bearing young from deserting the big city and concentrating their interests in the suburbs; if we are bemused by each educational whim (and thereby encourage more whims); if we pay little personal attention to languages, mathematics and classical studies; if we enthuse over formica lunch counters and forget Plato and Tacitus; if we run benefits for drum majorettes' uniforms and omit a raise for the physics teacher; if we get more excited about flying saucers than the evolution of Soviet technology if, in other words, we insist on being good-hearted, good-natured American citizens who would rather sit beside the TV with a can of beer than browse in Thoreau, then where does the blame lie for our youth crisis, our school crisis—on the educators, the youngsters or ourselves?]

In this kind of atmosphere we enshrine the shibboleth of universal education among the ikons. No one questions its value. Everyone assumes that it exists. No one notices that the schools of New York and most metropolitan cities actually act as mere custodial agents for a substantial group of children who are just waiting for the legal age in order to leave school. No real effort is made to educate these youngsters. The law says they must sit in school. So sit in school they do unless they are clever enough to work the "continuation school" dodge, the "doctor's certificate" dodge or simply decide to truant (thereby winning the unspoken gratitude of the school which was saddled with their presence).] New York and most metropolitan school systems have installed a number of "tracks." Some of these tracks are traveled by bright youngsters. They lead to college. Some are traveled by average youngsters. They lead to a trade—radio repairman, beauty operator. And some lead nowhere. The poor, plodding, unfit youngster is simply kept inside four walls from 8:30 in the morning to 3 P.M. five days a week. He does nothing. He is capable of doing little. He is serving time. When he leaves school he gets a certificate. It means nothing except that he has been too timid to become a truant.

Is universal education really possible? What is our purpose in confining a physically mature, nonintellectual boy eager to start on a job and begin his adult life to two or three more years of school?

Different children have different capacities, different chronological ages for maturation. Everyone knows this. But we ask the schools to blind themselves and treat all pupils as though they were equal in learning capability. We take a sound general concept like universal education and torture it into a ritualistic absolute.

A corollary of the universal education principle is the child labor act. Children are not permitted to work before they are sixteen or, in some categories, before they are eighteen. A fine social principle. One which progressive men and women fought long and hard to establish. It was designed to end the tragedy of the "breaker" boy and the thirteen-year-old girl of the loft factories. Every good law has a dark side but only a few iconoclasts are bold enough to challenge so hallowed a principle as the ban on child labor. The ban has killed the apprentice system. It has give labor unions a vast interest in keeping the young out of the labor market. Yet, there are hundreds of thousands of youngsters ready to work, eager to work, in need of work, youngsters who can gain nothing more from school and yet are forced to sit at desks all day long. No wonder these youngsters become problems to themselves, to the schools, to a city.

What are needed, in Professor MacIver's opinion, are pre-vocational schools. If we insist on the boy serving out his days in school at least he can prepare himself for a trade. Regular education is impractical for such youngsters. They lack the capacity. But New York has no such system despite the great need of the delinquent youngsters. These are the boys who are screened out of regular vocational training.

Such courses would help. But why do not schoolmen raise the question of realistic interpretation of the universal education principle and the child labor laws and why do we not discuss a revival of the apprentice system? The answer seems to be that such proposals would tread on vested interests. They are politically infeasible. Changes might create a new source of cheap labor. Perhaps so. But it is not so difficult to police factories as it is to police streets. It is hard to believe the social consequences would be worse than those of the present system.

In summertime all our schools close down for three months of hibernation. Each year a three months' hiatus in education is decreed, as if a youngster's learning capacity was so feeble that it would be exhausted without twelve weeks of hot-weather rest.

Not often will you hear an educator's voice challenge this anachronism, which survives from the day when America was a peasant country and the children were needed for farm chores (in Russia youngsters are still freed from school and mobilized for spring planting and fall harvesting). The three months' summer vacation is sheer waste. Expensive school installations stand idle, children rove the streets and get into trouble, schoolteachers take on extra jobs to eke out their low pay, habitually figured on a nine-months year. Summer is the season when delinquency habits are established. There is no more reason for the long summer vacation today than there is for planting cabbage only in the sign of the new moon.

In view of the problems which we face with our young people and the educational system, you would expect to hear violent, impassioned debate of these and other issues. The fact that you do not is one more symptom of the deep malaise of our society. True public debate, free flow of ideas, radical challenge of fixed concepts has vanished in the organizational stratification and specialization of society.

As Dr. Schweitzer long since noted:

"Another hindrance to civilization is the over-organization of our public life. . . . Personality and ideas are subordinated to institutions when it is really these which ought to influence the latter and keep them inwardly alive. . . .

"Thus, we have entered a new medieval period. The general determination of society has put freedom of thought out of fashion."

When all of this has been said in criticism it would be gross distortion not to record that, compared with other agencies of society, the schools are doing a vastly superior job with the young people and their problems. They could do much better. But they could also do far worse.

As Principal Levin pointed out: "Even the poorest school and the worst teacher is more concerned about the kid than any other agency." There is no question that next to a good family a good school best copes with the inadequate, bewildered adolescent. There is no one-shot, sure cure for delinquency. But if a community wants the quickest, cheapest, most effective results the place to spend money is in the school system. We sometimes forget that it is the business of school people to deal with children. They are experts at it. Here is the place, if there is one, to come to grips with the shook-up generation.

The New York schools are no model. But, as Professor Clark points out, they have one great virtue. Local autonomy is king. Each principal is as much the master of his school as the captain is master of his ship. This means there is an infinite variety of schools in New York. Some are very good. Some are better than you will find anywhere else.

There are not many teachers like the one who reported she had a little Puerto Rican girl who could hear but could not speak. An interpreter found that the little girl had been told she would be thrown out of school if she didn't pronounce the words correctly. She was playing it safe by not opening her mouth.

There are many more schools like that run by Mr. Levin, where it is recognized that Puerto Rican children present special problems because they have not been run through the stereotype of mass culture like American youngsters.

"The Puerto Rican youngster," Mr. Levin explained, "is much more individualistic than our children. He takes criticism very personally. He doesn't expect to be bawled out like our kids. He finds it hard to understand the importance we place on time. He is not used to precision—to being at places at a particular time.

"These youngsters, often, are not ready for the conformity which we insist on. The frustration which they encounter is enormous. Father and mother are working. They are taking care of baby. Baby has to be diapered. So they diaper it. And this makes them late for school.

"We reprimand them for being tardy. They reply—what difference does it make? If I don't do my lesson today, I will do it tomorrow. What is wrong with that?"

Lack of time sense is not unique to Puerto Ricans. Many minorities possess it. A school which understands the psychology of its pupils will do a good job of helping them with adjustment. As a Negro teacher put it in discussing the segregation problem in the New York schools: "I think our primary job is to see that we have such a good school and such good teachers that everyone is eager to come, regardless of color."

Joseph Noethen, an assistant superintendent in Brooklyn, believes that integration involves far more than making schools equally free to youngsters of all colors. True integration concerns deep areas of tradition, culture, mores. Negro and white children have little knowledge of the African culture of the Negro strains which make up the American colored community. Brooklyn Museum has set up a beautiful exhibition of African folk life and artifacts. All children of Mr. Noethen's district (there are Mohawk, Canarsie and Shinnecock Indian children, Filipinos and Indonesians as well as white and Negro in the district) are taken to the museum. They see for themselves what the roots and traditions of the Negro are like.

"Our Negro pupils need this as much, if not more, than the white children," Mr. Noethen feels. Part of the Negro's rootlessness stems from ignorance of his ethnic heritage. In the Soviet Union the same technique is employed for instilling pride and national feeling in culturally backward tribes and minor nationalities.

The Brooklyn Museum with its imaginative exhibits and programs demonstrates how such institutions can direct their facilities to help youngsters to relate better to each other and to the world.

One afternoon, Eugene Brice, a Negro baritone, was giving a concert at the museum. The hall was filled with schoolchildren. A group of obstreperous boys came in, looking for trouble. They sat in the rear of the hall and quieted gradually. As they left at the end of the concert one of them said to a nervous museum official: "This place is all right, mister. Sure, we're a gang. But we'll never cause any trouble in your joint."

One of the hotly debated aspects of the New York school system is what is called "600" schools. The name comes from the numerical series used to designate special schools set up to deal with the worst products of the shook-up age, the behavior cases, chronic truants, intractable boys who cannot be handled in general schools. The "600" schools are controversial because many educators who approve the general concept feel that those which have been created fall short of minimum requirements. They are said to be deficient in staff, sparsely equipped with psychological, psychiatric and other technical facilities. Professor MacIver found that a high percentage of youngsters who passed through the schools simply fell back into some other institution and that many youngsters continued their delinquency outside of the hours they were attending the "600" school.

"Their pattern of delinquency and gang connections remains the same," he said. "There is a tendency to refer youngsters at an age when they are already confirmed delinquents and resistant to change. The social mortality rate is terrific."

Professor MacIver's observations have sound basis. On the other hand there is no better place to observe what an intelligent, sensitive schoolman can do to help upset youngsters and assist them toward socially approved patterns than to go to one of these much criticized schools—P.S. 613 in Brooklyn.

Here is a school entirely populated by members of the shook-up generation. It is directed by a principal who understands these youngsters perfectly. You will hear no talk from Sidney I. Lipsyte about school housekeeping. His talk is about boys.

"Here," he said, "a boy is accepted as a boy in his own right. In another school he is just another bad boy—and gets kicked out. Here he is just a boy. We set up situations in which he can succeed. He carves a puppet or paints a picture. He can say: 'That's mine.' Nobody here is a failure."

To the kind of youngsters I met in the Brooklyn candy stores to find a place where you are not a failure must seem something like paradise.

The first thing which the youngsters learn is that they have no reason to get angry with the teachers. These boys have been subjected to much buffeting. Eighty-five per cent come from broken homes. They have been reprimanded repeatedly by teachers, principals and truant officers. Most of them have had trouble with the police. A third of them have been through Children's Court. They have had plenty of time to develop resentment against society. When they first arrive they are very quiet. Their eyes are watchful, apprehensive. When nothing bad happens to them for a few days they begin to test the limits of indulgence. They say and do things to see the reaction.

"They are surprised to find that while we don't approve of bad conduct, we don't reject them. We are firm but not angry," Mr. Lipsyte said.

These are children largely from slums. Their families, if any, are afflicted with alcoholism or criminality. The adults may be old, infirm, ill. They lack competence in dealing with youngsters. The boys seldom have been to church. They belong to gangs. From an early age they have been filled with anxiety, fear, tension, insecurity. These are not baseless anxieties and fears. The tension is real. So is the insecurity. They do not know how they will live from day to day. They are always on the move, every few weeks a new "home." They are passed from mother to grandmother, from aunt to friend. No one really wants them.

"You know," Mr. Lipsyte observed, "the youngster is generally better than he should be, considering his background. He is often a rejected child and he is made well aware of it. He may represent to his mother the image of a father who has deserted. He may stand in the way of a mother building a new life. He may be passed over for newer children. I have had a guardian bring a boy in and say: 'Put him in a home. You do it. We can't handle him.' How do you think a boy reacts to that kind of rejection?"

If Mr. Lipsyte could take the boys earlier, he agrees, he could do more with them. If a boy has been deteriorating for twelve or thirteen years it may be too late to help much. Yet, he thinks most boys are the better for their experience in his school. He believes that 90 per cent of them become useful citizens. He does not apply conventional middle-class standards to them. An arrest is not necessarily a clue to success or failure with these boys. In the milieu in which they live there are many arrests. If a boy grows up, gets a job, gets married and stays out of serious trouble, Mr. Lipsyte counts that a success.

After a youngster has been in school awhile he usually wants to talk over his problems.

"They must be listened to with intelligence," Mr. Lipsyte said. "Kids are getting better when they want to talk it over. The teacher must understand this. Adolescence is a period of storm and stress for all youngsters. They are growing up, they want to be independent, they do not have the resources for it."

There is a Boy Scout troop at Public School 613. At first Boy Scouts were regarded as sissies by the street boys who make up the school population. Only a few boys joined, just one with a uniform. They went on Saturday hikes and cookouts. No matter what the weather, no matter how cold, how snowy, how rainy, the Scouts went out. They began to build a "rep" as tough guys. Bopping youngsters, tough members of the Chaplains, the Bishops, the Stonekillers, admitted that Scouts were not "chicken" after all. A year later the troop had sixteen members. Most of them had uniforms. Some of the Bishops and Stonekillers had joined up.

The problem of working with upset youngsters is not, after all, so complex and mysterious. What it principally requires is common sense, understanding and a good heart.

This is demonstrated most dramatically by the puppet club at P.S. 613. The boys fashion the puppets themselves. They invent their own puppet shows. To listen to one is an experience. Puppets can say what they please about teachers, about other pupils, about fathers and mothers. They can say all the things that would get a boy in trouble if he said them himself. The boys use their puppets to act out their resentments. They have a wonderful time. No one interferes. When they have got it off their chests they feel much better.

The boys prepared a puppet program to present at a city-wide Boy Scout meet. They started with a skit full of suggestive jokes. The principal character was a TV salesman who cheated his customers, seduced their wives, and spent all his money on liquor. Everything that might possibly shock the teachers was put into the play. The teachers offered no comment. Gradually, the joke wore off. The character of the program changed. In the end it featured puppets playing bongo drums and singing Negro spirituals, the Beatitudes and the Lord's Prayer.

"You must not be too quick nor too severe in judging these

boys," Mr. Lipsyte emphasizes. He recalled a boy who threw a brick at a teacher three years ago. The boy would have been sent to an institution but had to be kept on because no place was open to him. Suddenly he started to read. He became a compulsive reader. He read and read and read. Nothing stopped him. Mr. Lipsyte brought in a psychiatrist who began to work with the boy. Within a short while the youngster entered night school. He took the examinations and entered the Printing Trades school, where he is maintaining a good average. The chances are that this youngster is going to find a useful place for himself in society.

It is clear that Mr. Lipsyte and many other teachers and educators have not taken the "path to inhumanity" which Dr. Schweitzer fears. There are in the schools, just as there are in society as a whole, individuals who are working with warmth and intelligence to protect and develop our younger generation. But they are working against odds. I think Mr. Noethen is right when he says: "We have come into a money era. If it sells, if it makes money—that is what counts. TV sells the toothpaste habit by picturing a long succulent kiss on the screen. This is good salesmanship. It sells toothpaste. It also arouses a primitive primeval desire in a boy. He makes a pass at a girl. This produces delinquency. Who is to blame?"

It is unrealistic to dissociate the problem of youth from the atmosphere in which youth lives. The youngsters are the products of American culture. So are the schools they attend. If the content of our culture is largely plastic, bleached wood pulp, chrome, acetate fiber and fresh frozen concentrates there is going to be much that is synthetic in the schools. If we insist on change and newness at the expense of value and principle our standards are bound to be as fleeting as styles in women's hats. If we measure ourselves in terms of Cadillacs rather than of Socrates the schools will turn out mechanics and auto buyers, not philosophers. It is not accident

but choice which causes new schools to resemble fun.
designed factories rather than academic halls.

If we do not like the product of our educational sys.
if its inadequacies are beginning, perhaps, to endanger ou
national security, we have only ourselves to blame. We
created the system in the pretty polyethylene image of the
culture which we reverence.

II

the street club worker

ONE winter evening, just at dusk, Abe Taylor was standing in the lobby of the Harlem Boys' Club, a neighborhood center connected with a big East Harlem public housing project. A crowd of teen-age boys was coming in the door when the crack of rifle fire rang out. Three boys fell, two of them critically wounded. The third stumbled through the door and died.

The rifle was fired by a boy sniper who had sat for an hour in a child's "jungle" of bars and ladders in a playground across the street from the center, his rifle concealed under his winter coat. In the confusion he escaped and was never apprehended.

Mr. Taylor was then twenty-nine years old and director of physical activities at the club. He had a B.S. degree from Agricultural and Technical College, a Negro school at Greensboro, North Carolina, a master's degree from the University of Minnesota, a second master's from New York University and was taking more graduate work at the New York School of Social Work.

Mr. Taylor is one of eleven children (four boys and seven girls) of a Baptist minister and his wife. All eleven children are college graduates. Mr. Taylor was born in Rocky Mount,

North Carolina, spent his childhood in North Carolina towns where his father preached and grew up to be a pretty good athlete "although I wasn't quite heavy enough for football."

The murderous shooting at the Boys' Club probably had much to do with finally determining the course which Mr. Taylor's career was to take. His interest had been divided for a long time between athletics and social work. He spent most of his Army career as a recreation officer in the Aleutians, assigned to an island close to those held by the Japanese. He had been trained for service in the South Pacific and so, naturally, the Army sent him to a north Pacific island where snow stayed on the ground the year around. The island was small, dismal and damp. There were no women on it. Many of the troops spent a year or eighteen months there without relief. The task of a recreation lieutenant was not easy. It was in the Aleutians that Mr. Taylor took up boxing. He had played basketball and football in college.

When he returned to college after the war he entered intercollegiate boxing and marked up a record of twelve wins and two draws before he graduated. He contemplated going into the ring professionally but was discouraged by Jersey Joe Walcott, a relative of his by marriage. Walcott pointed out that even if Mr. Taylor was successful in the ring his career would be short and he would be left without provision for his middle and old age. Mr. Taylor still had difficulty in picking his career as is shown by the fact that he spent three years at Minnesota getting a graduate degree in recreation and almost immediately entered New York University to get a graduate degree in health education.

At the Boys' Club Mr. Taylor's interests began to crystal-lize. Several gang groups used the club, among them the Enchanters and the Englishmen. These were highly structured gangs. Boys were put through a formal initiation of which the principal feature was hand-to-hand combat. When the youngsters found that Mr. Taylor could box and knew jujitsu they begged for instruction. This laid the foundation of an interest which now finds expression in the thesis which Mr. Taylor is preparing for his doctorate at N.Y.U. on the subject of physical education as it relates to the total development of the individual.

With his deepening interest in adolescents Mr. Taylor became attracted by the program of the New York City Youth Board. The Youth Board program is what is called "aggressive group work" or the "seeking out technique." This means that instead of sitting in offices, clinics or settlement houses and waiting for youngsters to come and ask for help, the Youth Board goes out onto the street, finds the youngsters who are in trouble or are potential sources of trouble, and begins to work with them right in the neighborhood. The Youth Board worker goes to the street corner where the kids hang out and hangs out with them. He goes to the ice-cream parlor where they loaf and loafs with them. He learns to talk their language, understand their interests and share their complicated life and its often insoluble problems.

The street club program, instituted when the agency was set up ten years ago because of concern over the growth of antisocial gangs, is not unique. The technique has been tried in some other cities, notably Los Angeles, but nowhere has it been developed so thoroughly as in New York City.

The Board now maintains about seventy workers on the streets. They work with perhaps eighty gangs and are in contact with a total of one hundred. This represents only a fraction of the known gangs in New York but a very high percentage of those which are actively antisocial. Captain Frederick Ludwig, the able chief of the New York Police Department's Juvenile Aid Bureau, estimates that there are not more than eight or nine thousand really dangerous youngsters in the whole city. The number of youngsters grouped into one kind of gang or another runs into six figures. But only a few gangs are antisocial. For instance, a careful survey of East Harlem disclosed about one thousand teen-age groupings or gangs. Only one hundred of these had engaged in any activity which had been noted by the police or Youth Board. Ten were regarded as "major conflict" groups. One or two of these contained very disturbed youngsters.

However, maps of the city show a disturbing spread of antisocial gangs, particularly from deteriorated areas into middle-class regions and from the center of the city out toward the periphery and the suburbs. The Youth Board concentrates its activity in fifteen primary areas of the city where conditions are believed to be worst. It shifts its workers as a general shifts his troops when the threat waxes in one place and wanes in another.

The Board is a small agency. Its annual budget is only $4,500,000, about half provided by the city and half by the state. It does not confine its activity to the streets. It advances funds to schools and community centers for special programs in difficult neighborhoods. It encourages community and volunteer efforts to strengthen neighborhood social structures. It tries to ease the tension surrounding the big new public housing projects. It finds money for special situation social studies.

But its trail-blazing work is with the street club project. This program has achieved major social results. But, perhaps because of its unorthodox nature, the street club activity has aroused bitter antagonism, especially from certain elements of the community which share much responsibility for stimulating delinquency and adolescent antagonisms toward the social system—the "nightstick" advocates within and without the Police Department, yellow newspaper editorialists who demand that the children be treated like beasts

("You wouldn't try social work on a tiger in the jungle, would you?"), and other citizens whose first reaction in a state of panic is always to reach for a stick or a gun.

There are those who complain that Youth Board work is hampered by red tape, that the leadership of its director, Ralph Whelan, lacks distinction, that it trims its sails to the political winds and that the professional standards of its workers are not what they should be. There is some justice in these criticisms. The board pays street club workers only $3,750, and senior workers $4,500. It operates on a shoestring (more than a quarter of its funds go to the Board of Education to finance school play centers). It finds it difficult to recruit and keep personnel for the fascinating but arduous task of street work.

The street worker's day begins about six in the evening and ends around midnight if there is no rumble or alert in his neighborhood. He is on duty every weekend because weekends are the time when the trouble starts. He spends long hours hanging around cold corners and dingy stores with difficult and unpredictable adolescents. Sometimes real danger is involved. More often his good work may be undone by factors beyond his control—bureaucratic intervention by other city agencies, brutalizing by the police, expulsions by housing authorities, suspensions by the School Board.

But no one challenges the obvious fact that Youth Board workers are out on the active front in the fight on juvenile delinquency, that they are among the few persons who work at first hand, night after night, to keep youngsters out of trouble and try to move them over to more socially approved ways of conduct.

It was this direct-action approach which attracted Mr. Taylor. In 1955 he applied for and obtained a position as a senior street club worker. His first assignment was to what he describes as "the most notorious, biggest acting-out gang group in Brooklyn," the Uptown Chaplains.

Mr. Taylor is a man with an almost histrionic ability to reproduce the "sound" of the street gangs. He can imitate their street corner slouch or their bopping demeanor. Like most effective street club workers he has a warm heart and a real affection for the hard-surfaced, dangerous-acting but oddly childlike young men he has tried to help. He feels both the humor and the pathos of the shook-up generation.

Mr. Taylor has not forgotten the night he met the Chaplains. He was taken to the street corner where the gang hung out by a club worker whose job he was assuming. The leader was a boy named Sam, only fifteen and a half, but that very day he had been in court, awaiting a hearing in a murder case. He was not the boy who had done the killing. Mr. Taylor learned later, but he carried the gun which was used. Sam was a dynamic youngster. He talked with great enthusiasm. He ruled the gang with an iron hand. What he said went. Mr. Taylor met about twenty-five of the youngsters that night, standing under a street light. It was his first exposure to a street gang.

The next night he was on his own. He went down to the corner. The boys were all there. He felt an atmosphere of suppressed excitement which he did not understand. Sam asked him to have a drink of wine. Mr. Taylor refused. The bottle was passed around.

"It was my first night," Mr. Taylor recalls. "I had no relationship with the kids. Sam said to me, 'We're going now, but don't follow us. Just wait here.' He didn't say they were going to fight, to go down on someone. But I noticed the boys were wearing gloves. They had their leather jackets on. They went off and I watched which way they took. They went toward the Bishops' neighborhood. I called my supervisor and said it looked to me like there was going to be a rumble."

One boy had stayed back. He was a kid named Wimpy. Mr. Taylor asked him where the others were going but he

wouldn't say. Mr. Taylor asked the boy if he could walk him
back home. The boy said sure.

"I asked him why he had stayed back," Mr. Taylor said.
"He told me he didn't mind hanging out. But he just didn't
want to get into any trouble."

As they walked down the street Mr. Taylor was surprised
to notice the boy take off his hat and put it solemnly over his
heart.

"That's the house where Joe lived," Wimpy said. "He
was a member of the gang who was killed. It is a rule of the
gang. When you pass the home of a member who has died you
put your hat over your heart."

Three months later Sam was sent up to Warwick State
Training School for his part in the murder. The assistant
president, a boy named Chick, took over the gang. By this
time Mr. Taylor was at home with the boys. They knew him.
They depended upon him much more than they realized.
When he missed an evening on the street corner they became
alarmed. They joked and teased him but he had their confidence. They had accepted the three basic rules under which
a street worker attaches himself to a gang. They understood
that if Mr. Taylor saw them with a weapon he would call
on them to turn it over or inform the police. They understood that if he found them taking dope or suspected they
had narcotics on their person he would ask them to turn
it over and inform the authorities. And they knew that if
he learned they were going down or starting a gang fight he
would call in the police to try to halt it.

Outside of these ground rules they had learned that Mr.
Taylor, while never approving antisocial conduct, did not
set himself up a a judge or censor. If they had a problem with
the police, the court, with their school, a truant officer, the
probation officer, or even at home, they found Mr. Taylor
would help any way he could. If they wanted a job he would
try to find one for them.

On the basis of this confidence Mr. Taylor had begun to try to move the gang out of its narrow pattern of anti-social activity. He made little progress until Sam was sent away. Chick was different. He was attending a "600" school. He was one of fourteen youngsters in a family. His father was dead or had deserted the family. His mother was a cardiac case. Chick's family knew he was in the gang and tried to discourage him from it. His older brother used to beat him up every time he heard of Chick doing something with the gang.

Mr. Taylor got Chick to introduce him to his mother. He visited Chick's school and talked to his principal. He arranged to be informed every time Chick skipped school. Chick was good with his hands but had never had training in boxing. Mr. Taylor took him to the Police Athletic League center and began to teach him to box. Using Chick's passion for boxing he started to redirect the boy's interests and, through him, the interests of the gang.

This was not easy. Chick got into trouble occasionally. Mr. Taylor watched his school attendance like a hawk. Finally, Chick graduated from school. Mr. Taylor bought him a graduation present. Chick wanted to go on to regular high school but he didn't have the qualifications. Mr. Taylor persuaded him to get a job instead, and enroll in classes in continuation school. Chick got a job, paying sixty dollars a week.

"You should have seen what it did to his pride," Mr. Taylor says. "He had been poor as a church mouse. If he wanted a cigarette he had to ask me for a cigarette. Now, he came up, pulled out a pack and said, 'Man, have a cigarette. Have one of mine.' "

Chick's conduct broke more and more from the pattern of the gang. The group began to display anger and uncertainty. Their leader was no longer leading them. They felt lost. Some gang members wanted to follow Chick. Others knew no other way of life than the old bopping habits.

Mr. Taylor was not certain how well he had done with Chick until a crisis arose. Chick was laid off. It would have been easy to go back to the old gang ways. Chick didn't. He hunted up another job at a little better pay. Mr. Taylor then knew he had reclaimed a boy from the streets.

"He's gone Ivy League now," Mr. Taylor chuckles. "He's no Chaplain any more. He brushes his hair back and cuts it short. He's stopped wearing a hat."

This result was not achieved without concentrated efforts. The main direction of Mr. Taylor's work and of the Youth Board workers, in general, is to try to broaden the terribly limited horizon of these boys. Many of the youngsters seldom left an area of four or six blocks around the gang hangout. Mr. Taylor found that they did not go to the movies often because they had to cross the territory of two or three other gangs and were afraid of being attacked.

He took them to movies in Manhattan. He even took them to a play or two but, he admits, that was an experiment that failed. The boys were bored. They liked the movies better. He took them to see the Columbia University campus. "Man, this is a home," the youngsters commented. A "home" is the ultra in street argot. The youngsters were astonished to see that boys who could well afford hats went bareheaded. The prestige which the boys attach to hats, the eagerness with which they spend fifteen or twenty dollars if they get it for a hat intrigues Mr. Taylor. The hat is obviously intimately associated with status. Possibly it is a symbol which comes to them from peasant antecedents. The Russian peasant associates the hat with the white-collar class and "culture." A common street reprimand heard in Moscow is: "How can you be so uncultured, you, who are wearing a hat!"

Mr. Taylor is no longer a street club worker. He supervises a large and difficult area of Brooklyn for the Youth Board. He is working hard on his doctorate. At thirty-four he has been too busy with his studies and his gangs to get married.

"However," he says, "I haven't been a creep. I do get to see a play or an opera now and then and I go to two or three dances a year."

He is a neatly dressed man with a liking for three-button gray flannel suits, dark ties and neat white handkerchiefs in his breast pocket. He wears horn-rimmed glasses. He belongs to the Methodist Church. He is convinced that the Youth Board is doing the most challenging social work in the city and is fascinated to be participating in it. His hobby is jazz. He has a hi-fi and a good collection of Dave Brubeck and George Shearing.

"I like jazz," he said. "The modern kind. I like it cool."

Another man who likes it cool is Aaron Schmais. Mr. Schmais is a little younger than Mr. Taylor. He is just thirty, married six years and the father of a four-year-old girl named Beth and a nine-month-old boy named Michael.

Mr. Schmais is also a Youth Board supervisor who started as a street club worker. He is a native New Yorker who grew up in the Bronx in an area which has recently become the scene of a good deal of gang activity. When he was a kid it was a quiet, lower-middle-class Jewish neighborhood without gangs. There was some stealing and vandalism but weapons were not common and fighting was not an important part of adolescent activity. Now many of the Jewish families have moved out. Puerto Ricans are moving in, most of the social facilities have followed their Jewish sponsors to the suburbs and the neighborhood is headed for trouble.

Mr. Schmais, like Mr. Taylor, drifted into youth activity through an interest in sports. Mr. Schmais's sport is basketball. He spent several summers at Catskill resorts as an athletic director and played on neighborhood New York teams, often as the only white player on a team made up of

Negroes. Mr. Schmais went to DeWitt Clinton High School in New York, attended City College for two semesters, then switched to Oswego State Teachers College, where he got his B.S. in 1950. Two years later he took a degree in psychology at Long Island University and now he is working on a social work master's degree at New York School of Social Work. Almost all of the Youth Board workers are young. They are college-trained people. Most of them are taking advanced studies of one sort or another. The street worker's hours offer some attraction to graduate students since their days are largely free for study.

Mr. Schmais started as a teacher in a fine private junior high school in Westchester. But he continued to play basketball in Manhattan on Sundays and one of his close friends was working for the Youth Board. Through this friend he met Hugh Johnson, then in charge of a tough Harlem area for the Youth Board. In 1953 Mr. Schmais quit his teaching job, took a $600 salary cut and went to work with a difficult gang, then active in the vicinity of 105th Street between Park and Lexington avenues. This gang was made up, for the most part, of Puerto Rican youngsters, living in a predominantly Italian neighborhood.

Mr. Schmais found that the leader of the gang was an unusual boy named Rico. This youngster was the most successful kid in the neighborhood. He was a dope pusher. Some weeks he made as much as $200. He used his influence in some surprising ways. He persuaded the gang members to stop bopping because he was afraid it would bring on police intervention and interfere with his drug sales. He flatly refused to sell dope to boys and kicked out of the gang any kid who started to use drugs. He sold only to adults. With his money he bought jackets for the gang, took care of hospital bills of members, paid for the rent on his mother's flat, paid most of the family expenses and sometimes spent sixty dollars to buy a coat as a present for one of his boys.

Rico was known throughout the neighborhood as an intelligent and clever boy. He never used drugs himself. Not long after Schmais attached himself to this group (having made the contact through another street club worker who knew some of the boys) Rico was arrested. There was a considerable delay before his case came before the court. In this time Mr. Schmais was able to persuade the boy to break his connections with the dope-peddling syndicate, to refuse the services of the syndicate lawyer and to accept an attorney provided by the Legal Aid Society.

He also got Rico to take back into the gang the youngsters he had kicked out and to work with them in trying to rehabilitate the drug users. Rico displayed as much energy and ingenuity in this as he had in the sale of drugs. Sometimes he stayed with a boy all day long and physically prevented him from getting any dope. Because of his thorough knowledge of addicts he was able to do much in getting some of the boys back toward normalcy.

"Of course," Mr. Schmais says, "this was only a limited help. We could not change the setup. No matter how many social workers you put into a neighborhood you are not doing any permanent good if the dope pushers are still there and all the rest of it. The neighborhood itself has got to change to make a difference permanently."

But Mr. Schmais was able to do a lot. He found his boys very much like Mr. Taylor's in their insularity. Only two boys in the group had ever been to the 86th Street movie houses—twenty blocks distant—because they had to cross other gang territories. Their first trip to 86th Street was as big an occasion for them as a trip to Europe for a Midwest businessman. Mr. Schmais gave them lectures on how to behave on the subway train, what to do when they came to the cashier's window at the movie house, and how to get Cokes out of a Coke machine.

Because the gang was giving up bopping it began to be

harassed by other gangs around the periphery of its turf. Mr. Schmais tried—not always with success—to show them how much more guts it took not to fight under provocation.

Rico was sentenced to a term of three years in the federal penitentiary. Mr. Schmais corresponded with him while he was in prison. He was released after a year and a half. He is now married and working. He makes sixty dollars a week and does not seem to miss the easy money of dope pushing. Mr. Schmais attended his wedding. Rico and his wife sometimes visit Mr. and Mrs. Schmais. Mrs. Schmais is also interested in work with youngsters. She is a playground director for handicapped youngsters with a master's degree in education.

"I remember the most serious talk I ever had with Rico," Mr. Schmais says. "I told him he had to face up to the facts. He had been arrested. He had to stop selling drugs. He listened to what I had to say. Then he fell asleep. It was some kind of a psychological escape mechanism. But when he woke up he gave me a solemn promise he would never sell dope again. He kept that promise."

Mr. Schmais is a youthful, serious man. He wears tweed suits, narrow-collared shirts, brown wool ties. The gang boys called him "Sosh" or "Aaron" or "Teach." Usually "Teach."

In December he and his wife spent their vacation in Puerto Rico. Like many New York social workers they want to learn more about the culture and the background of the Puerto Ricans before they come to El Barrio de Nueva York. Mr. Schmais speaks some high school Spanish and often was able to understand the gang youngsters when they switched from English to Spanish to keep their secrets from him.

The times Mr. Schmais likes most to remember about his work with the street boys are the late summer evenings after the centers and the ice-cream parlors had closed and things were quiet. Then he would go to the park, sometimes, with the boys. They would sit and talk about the things that kids always like to talk about, about life and religion and girls and what they would like to do. Once one of the boys got a telescope and brought it along.

"We sat and looked at the stars," Mr. Schmais recalls. "The kids wondered whether they could see any flying saucers. Then we got to talking about whether flying saucers really existed and whether there was life on Mars and on the moon. Things like that . . ."

Once you get under the surface, the same kind of questions interest the street boys as interest kids all over the world. Evenings like that, in the park, under the stars are hard to classify as social work technique. But they probably help to ease a youngster back onto the hard path of social purposefulness more than a policeman's billy or even an expensive program of social agency activity.

Not all the young men who work for the New York Youth Board are as humane and understanding and able as Mr. Taylor and Mr. Schmais. But many are. There is, however, one real fault to be charged against these street club workers. It is simply put. There are not enough of them.

12

the churches

ONE of the first places I visited in my inquiry into street gang life was a barren store building in the heart of Bedford-Stuyvesant. Bedford-Stuyvesant is a sprawling area in central Brooklyn which until a generation ago was a lower-middle-class white residential section. Less than twenty years ago a spillover of Negro families from Harlem began and the area sank into blight and depression. The corner store which I visited had been remodeled into a "lounge" by the New York Youth Board. It is reached by driving through a wilderness of slum houses, streets lined with liquor stores, pentecostal churches, saloons and dimly lighted dives. You are seldom long out of sight of a prowl car.

The corner occupied by the lounge is as dismal as any in the area. Behind a cheap new façade the beaverboard partitions of the entrance hall are torn and broken. The office walls are so flimsy that they sway at a touch. Some interior windows have been broken, others are replaced with cardboard.

On the Friday night of my visit a dance was in progress and a young man was collecting tickets (twenty-five cents a head) at a table near the door. The room was in half darkness but I could see that the floor was of linoleum tile and the walls of bare cement blocks which had been painted lavender up to shoulder height and left unpainted above that. Across the ceiling half a dozen twisted strands of yellow and red crepe paper had been stretched. There seemed to be fifty or sixty young people in the room, most of them Negro boys sixteen to eighteen years old. There were fifteen or twenty girls. I saw only one white boy. The room was barren of furniture. About fifteen couples were dancing to the quiet rhythms being played on a portable phonograph, most of them "fishing." Some girls were dancing together. The majority of the boys seemed to be wandering about a bit aimlessly, standing in groups silently, or talking casually. All wore their half- or three-quarter-length light spring coats. It was cold in the room. I noticed two girls of about sixteen who were wearing identical white-and-gray plaid slacks.

About four staff members were present, including a broadshouldered man who was in charge of the lounge. A policeman lolled in an inner office, a nightstick dangling in his hand from a leather thong.

The director said, with some pride, that the boys had decorated the lounge themselves, that they had provided the record player and records, and organized the sale of tickets. He also pointed out that all had removed their hats, that their language was fairly restrained and that no one, so far at least, had gotten noticeably drunk.

It was plain from the director's conversation that even such a simple task as stringing crepe paper, removing the pingpong tables and setting up the room for a dance was a signal accomplishment in terms of these youngsters' social capability. He interrupted his conversation several times to follow boys into the toilet, located just off the dance floor. The youngsters were drinking in there and he was trying to discourage this. He apologized for the general appearance of the lounge, explaining that a few months ago some youngsters had broken in over a weekend, stolen the television set, smashed the windows, torn down compoboard walls and, in general, wrecked the place. The lounge was closed for several weeks and only recently had reopened. There was little money for repairs and they had to make do as best they could.

I could hardly understand why the youngsters would use such poor facilities but the director explained there was simply no place in the neighborhood for them to go. There are several community centers, some distance away, including an excellent one run by Dr. Gardner Taylor's Concord Baptist Church and another by St. Peter Claver Catholic Parish. But they are too far for most of the youngsters. Two or three nights a week the lounge shows an old western movie (most of these boys are too poor to go to the movies and there are no TV's in their homes). Other nights the kids play ping-pong or cards or listen to the radio until ten o'clock closing time.

"There is literally no other place for them to go," the director said. "These youngsters have been picked up by the police so often, beaten up and pushed around so much that they are badly cowed. They are glad to have any place where they can get off the street, where no one will use a nightstick on them."

The director explained that the dance would go on until midnight, that it undoubtedly would be peaceful, outside of a few drunks, so long as no gang boys from outside the neighborhood tried to crash in.

"We will stay around until well after midnight," he said of his staff, "to make sure the boys and their girls get off the streets and home safe."

Outside of a few Russian provincial villages I do not think I have ever seen a more dreary "recreation" facility than the Bedford-Stuyvesant lounge. Yet in the wilderness in which these poverty-stricken young people live it is sufficiently better than their normal surroundings to seem attractive.

No one can visit the lounge and walk the streets of Bedford-Stuyvesant without appreciating the truth of the statement of

the Reverend Jerry Oniki of Harlem's fine Church of the
Master.

"The church and the synagogue are not living up to their
responsibility," he believes. "The church has a heavy responsibility. Not just to its own congregation but to the geographical area in which it is located. The churches have not
lived up to this responsibility. Most of them concentrate on
their own members."

He points to Bedford-Stuyvesant as a prime example of
the failure of the churches and church-sponsored and church-
supported social agencies to meet urgent needs away from
their own locales.

"Who will put the community centers into the areas that
need them, Bedford-Stuyvesant, for example?" he asks. "No
one. It is difficult to get central planning in social work just
as it is difficult to get it in the expansion of the city. It just
does not exist. No one sits down with a map and thinks about
what the city should be like, how it can be improved. The
city grows like Topsy. Everything in it has a separate life.
We all have to pay for the horrible cancers which we all
create."

A few institutions are doing fine work in Bedford-Stuyvesant. Dr. Gardner Taylor's church is one. There are
others. But the harsh fact is that most of the spiritual needs
of this great slum are relegated to the pentecostal pastors,
themselves often living on the thin edge of starvation. No
one cares whether Bedford-Stuyvesant lives with God or
devil. No one cares whether there is a place for the children
of the streets or whether they are clobbered night after night
by men who cannot understand that these blows merely condition a new generation to hatred for the civilization into
which they were born.

Bedford-Stuyvesant is only one of many areas in New York
in which the churches have rejected their true responsibilities.
You will find the same situation in every great city of the

country, particularly as more and more churches pull up stakes from older neighborhoods and join the exodus to the suburbs.

In the Claremont area of the Bronx last spring occurred one of the season's more spectacular youth gang killings. A gang adolescent named Michael Ramos was shot and killed in a candy store. A young gang leader named Ramon Serra, twenty, was arrested in the shooting. The case aroused particular interest because Ramos had been in the public eye previously as a witness in the trial of the seven boys who were accused of slaying Michael Farmer, a half-crippled boy, in a teen-age rumble.

The area in which Ramos was shot provides a classic example of what happens to a section of the city when the population shifts and social services provided by church or religious groups move out. This had been largely a Jewish neighborhood with some Italians. Most of the residents came from the lower East Side and worked in the garment trades. There were two good social agencies, Bronx House, a settlement house financed by Jewish funds, and the Fulton Street Young Men's Hebrew Association.

A few years ago the neighborhood began to change. Jewish families started moving farther up in the Bronx and to the suburbs. An influx of Puerto Ricans and Negroes began. Five years ago the City Housing Authority announced plans for a large slum-clearance project in the area. The exodus of the old and influx of the new were speeded. Four years ago the YMHA moved out. It shifted its operations up to Grand Concourse. Bronx House stayed on until a year ago. Then it too moved up to Pelham Parkway. The Bronx House workers were worried about their withdrawal. They realized that serious social problems were developing and they managed to start a small neighborhood association before they left. It was an inadequate substitute but it was all they could do.

Gang activity developed rapidly. But there was no one to halt it. Finally, the Youth Board, sensing trouble ahead, began to move. Indeed, a new Youth Board worker spent the very day of the shooting in the company of Serra and some of his gang companions, trying to lay the basis of a permanent association with the group. At the moment the shooting occurred, the worker, a young university student, was within a few feet of the spot. Had he been assigned earlier he might have prevented a boy's death. It was too little and too late.

This case illustrates what too often happens. Just at the moment when the social needs of a neighborhood begin to increase the existing agencies, tied to church groups, move out. Bronx House, by fateful coincidence, had been located directly opposite the candy shop where Ramos was shot.

There is another failure which must be charged to the churches. This is the failure of church facilities in a changing environment to utilize their resources effectively. Some even blunder into policies which sharpen the lines of conflict in a community.

I have mentioned that community centers sometimes close their doors to all youngsters except those of a particular gang or gangs. This is done in the name of "avoiding trouble" or excluding "rough boys" or preventing vandalism. This policy, in effect, turns the settlement house into a base for a particular gang. A room may be set aside for gang meetings. This is done with good intentions. It is supposed to acclimate the gang to a social rather than an antisocial life. But when a segment of the neighborhood is invited inside the center and another segment is kept outside, the fighting and tension beyond the center's friendly walls almost certainly will increase.

I know of one area in New York, a region of considerable gang conflict, in which there are two youth facilities. One is a settlement house maintained by Protestant churches. The other is a Catholic Youth lounge in the local parish house. The neighborhood once was mostly Irish and Italian Catholic with a Protestant minority. Both facilities were open to all children. Then, the area began to change. Negro and Puerto Rican families came in. For a long time the Protestant center, for all practical purposes, barred Negro and Puerto Rican children. It provided a club room for an Italian gang and, tacitly, the gang controlled admission to the center. An Irish gang held the same position at the CYO center. The Negroes and Puerto Ricans had the use of the streets.

Finally, the Irish youngsters became too unruly and the parish priest barred them from the CYO center. They moved over to join the Italians in the Protestant center. The CYO stood almost unused. Although most of the incoming Puerto Rican children were Roman Catholic they were not made very welcome in the parish. Some residents commented bitterly that the priest didn't seem to like his new poor parishioners as well as his old more well-to-do ones.

Meanwhile, on the streets gang conflict flourished. The Irish and Italian youngsters fought it out against the new Negro and Puerto Rican arrivals. Finally the Irish and Italian boys grew so rough that the Protestant center barred them. But it did not admit Negro and Puerto Rican kids. It, too, was practically deserted. The Irish and Italian boys drifted back to the CYO, but the Father was stern. He often forbade them to use the gym for one reason or another. There were only two volunteer workers at the lounge and the youngsters were shooed out early.

Thus, neither Protestant nor Catholic facility was doing much for the neighborhood. If anything they had sharpened the division in the streets. Lately Puerto Rican and Negro youngsters have been admitted to the Protestant facility. In effect this gives the neighborhood two bases, two conflict groups. In neither case have the religious faiths recognized their real responsibility to the community. Each views the

problem from a narrow perspective. The churches are following policies which promote rather than restrain the
growth of delinquency.

Some Puerto Ricans feel that the Catholic churches in
New York do not yet live up to their responsibilities to their
Puerto Rican communicants. In the opinion of Madame
Encarnación Armas, for example, the Brooklyn diocese has
been particularly remiss in this respect. She agreed, however, that Cardinal Spellman is moving vigorously to see
that the church improves its work with Puerto Ricans. Many
priests are being sent to Puerto Rico to study Spanish and
Puerto Rican customs. The condition will improve with
time.

And, of course, some of the finest church work in the city
is that of the little Nativity Mission of Fathers Janer and
Hoodak in the Puerto Rican community on Forsyth Street.

Father Hoodak emphasizes again and again the impera-
tive need for more vigorous work by churches of all faiths
with the problem youngsters and problem neighborhoods.

"What so many of us fail to understand," he told me, "is
that this question of young people's behavior is largely a
moral one. When I mention morals the immediate reaction
of most people is—oh, there goes the Catholic Church again!
Trust a Jesuit to try to get a convert any way he can!
But that is not what I am talking about at all. These disturbed young people simply do not know the difference
between good and bad. They do not know what is evil. It
is a moral question. No one is training them in the funda-
mentals of human conduct. These are issues that are not
peculiar to Catholicism. They are peculiar to humanity."

The Nativity Mission does not discriminate between Catholic and non-Catholic.

"If we ask a child or a man if he is a Catholic or not,"
said Father Hoodak, "believe me we ask only so that if he
is a Catholic we can help him in his religion as well as in

his material needs. We do not turn anyone away. We help according to need and not according to faith."

Here just off the Bowery is a church which takes the whole world for its parish.

"I don't suppose one in ten of our clients comes from our parish," Father Hoodak says. "That isn't important. We are here to help people."

Father Janer in his cubbyhole mission offers a rare lesson to the mighty churchmen with their Park Avenue apartments, their fine stone buildings on upper Fifth Avenue, their best-selling books and their wealthy congregations. He offers a lesson, too, to some narrow-minded priests in poor neighborhoods who are more interested in keeping gymnasium floors clean than in keeping boys off the streets.

The Reverend George B. Ford, the retired parish priest of the Corpus Christi Roman Catholic Church on the edge of Harlem, puts the matter with his customary bluntness:

"We face a failure of society to assume its responsibilities. There is a failure of the churches to reach out and seize the opportunity which exists. We have segregation in the congregation—segregation by income as well as by color. Segregation in the congregation enhances segregation on the streets. Too many churches are guided by what is presumed to be the influence of their better-class parishioners."

What is said of the better-class church in New York City may be said of only too many better-class churches around the country. Not only do these churches repudiate the people who live in their vicinity but they blind themselves to conditions among the needy. Most churches find time and money for romantic, far-off missionary work. How many of them think of adopting the struggling little store-front church in the slum and sharing with it a little of their riches?

There are, of course, exceptions.

In New York City a group of churches of all faiths on the fashionable upper East Side have banded together in an organization called Interfaith Neighbors. They have put a street club worker into a neighborhood near where many of their fashionable members live and worship. In New York it is never too long a walk from riches to rags. Four blocks east of Park Avenue you can find conditions not too different from those of Bedford-Stuyvesant. One worker supported by a dozen churches does not seem like much. But it is a start.

Of the churches in New York which have assumed a responsibility for their fellowmen none can exceed the role being played by Trinity Episcopal Church, the famous spire at the head of Wall Street, a rich, venerable church with a rich, venerable list of patrons and members. Trinity Church has assumed stewardship for one of the worst areas of the lower East Side. The moving spirit of this work is the pastor of St. Augustine's Chapel, Father C. Kilmer Myers. I had heard of Father Myers long before I met him. His name is known widely for his courageous, dedicated work with the street gangs of the lower East Side.

It was raining the night I visited St. Augustine's Chapel, a steady late-April drizzle. There were not many people on the street as I made my way along East Broadway, past the offices of the *Jewish Daily Forward*, a block east to Henry Street. Henry Street is a dark slum street. Its asphalt pavement glistened in the softly falling rain and the wet ashcans at the curb reflected the light of the widely spaced street lamps. Two girls with rouged cheeks, holding a single plastic raincoat over their heads, chirped at me from the doorway where they stood, half in and half out of the rain. Although the street is poor there were cars parked almost bumper to bumper. Not shiny new cars. But still they were cars.

I walked down the street, passing a man with a worn brown overcoat hunched over his shoulders and carrying a half orange-crate in one hand, perhaps for a potbellied stove in one of the sagging ancient houses. I passed dimly lighted *bodegas* and other stores with Spanish names. Here and there were signs in Yiddish, Talmud Torahs, Hebrew charitable societies, relics of a culture and population which was fast being inundated. Suddenly, I found myself before a plain structure with a gray stone façade. It was St. Augustine's Chapel.

I had come to St. Augustine's for a specific purpose. A few nights earlier three of Father Myers' boys had appeared on a television program to tell about life on the streets and give their ideas of what the city might do with the problem. As a participant in a discussion which followed their appearance I had gotten acquainted with the boys.

Almost immediately after the TV appearance, one of the boys had been arrested in connection with a stabbing near St. Augustine's. The occurrence deeply upset the youngsters in the area. It also upset Father Myers, particularly the possibility of some connection between the TV program and the arrest. I knew that the police in Father Myers's parish were not friendly to him and that police hostility toward street work with the gangs was becoming increasingly vocal. Two youngsters whom I had written about had gotten into trouble with the police shortly after I wrote them up. There was no evidence of any connection. Still, I wondered whether there might be a pattern of deliberate efforts to try to discourage the street adolescents from associating with individuals who were trying to help them. If this was so it would be a serious indictment.

So when Father Myers told me that some of the boys were coming in to discuss things with him and asked me to attend I was quick to accept his invitation.

The conference, it developed, was an extremely serious one. Three boys took part, the most important of whom was a youngster nicknamed Reno, who had been a participant in the TV program. Reno is a highly articulate boy of about eighteen with much more insight than most adult New

Yorkers into conditions on the streets and their cause. He himself is a product of the streets. He knows what gang boys are like and how they react. He and his friends live south of St. Augustine's parish but have been using its facilities for some time at Father Myers' initiative. Father Myers has worked day and night to direct these youngsters toward sound social goals. The TV broadcast, in a sense, was a high-water mark which, it was hoped, would seal the transition of the group from street activity to the socialized pursuits of ordinary youngsters.

Reno was the key to this plan of Father Myers'. Reno had worked with great persistence to bring his friends into St. Augustine's. He was doing his best to direct their interests away from the streets. There had been some difficulty with the younger boys but by the evening of the broadcast everything seemed to be moving smoothly. Reno himself had completed school. He was interested in going on to college and Father Myers hoped that the TV show might reach someone who could make this ambition possible. I imagine that Father Myers also felt that the broadcast would help to make clear to the public as a whole the nature of what he was trying to do and, incidentally, to provide a rebuttal to those advocates of tough police action as an answer to the increasing disturbance of the street adolescents.

However, there is no easy road to success when you are dealing with difficult youngsters in a difficult milieu.

The broadcast was scheduled for a Friday evening. The three boys had recorded their part on film. A dance was scheduled at the chapel that night and the youngsters planned to gather beforehand and see themselves on TV. Father Myers was a little nervous about the combination of TV show and dance. He thought that might provide more excitement than was wise. He knew how unpredictable the youngsters could be. However, the boys promised there would be no trouble and the program went ahead.

All might have been well had it not been for a boy named Nickels. This boy was from an uptown neighborhood and what he was doing in the Henry Street area is not clear. At any rate he and a friend turned up at the dance, a little drunk.

The pair created some bad feeling. Some boys felt they had been rude and insulting. Reno kept the peace by insisting that it was just a matter of too many drinks and that the pair meant no harm. But after the dance the offenders got into a tussle with one of the Henry Street boys. They pushed him off the sidewalk and one drew a knife and cut the buttons off his new jacket.

Saturday night the boys gathered again. There was high feeling about Nickels and his companion. The evening ended with another minor fray in which one boy was slightly cut in the buttocks. On Sunday night one of the two alleged trouble-makers was spotted in the neighborhood. Some of the Henry Street boys jumped on him and before the fracas was over the boy had been badly knifed.

It was this occurrence which had led to the arrest of the boy Chico, who had appeared on the TV show. Chico had been routed out of bed in the middle of the night, warned not to try to contact Father Myers, taken to the hospital, where the wounded boy identified him, and then lodged in jail.

The boys were upset by a number of things. They asserted with a good deal of supporting evidence that Chico had had nothing to do with the knifing and that he had, in fact, been in St. Augustine's at the time, trying to find Reno in order to stop the trouble on the street. They felt that Chico's arrest had been deliberately made by the police "to get even" for the TV appearance, and they felt that these events had proved the impossibility of trying to break out of the eternal pattern of violence on the streets.

Reno acted as spokesman, talking with considerable eloquence. He is a rather handsome boy with high cheekbones, and under the impact of strong feeling his face works nervously as though he were about to cry. As he spoke he occasionally buried his face in his hands, then straightened up almost forcibly composing himself with a shake of his head.

He spoke about his friends of the street with emotion, told of the troubles they had had and of the high hopes with which they had accepted Father Myers' invitation to come in and make use of the chapel. He told of the expectations which he had had himself. But after the sudden and disheartening events of the past few days he did not feel there was any point in going on. It would only bring down trouble on everyone, on the boys, on the chapel, on Father Myers and his staff.

"The time has come to bust it up," he said. "There is no other way. We came up here and we entered into an agreement. We did our best and you did your best. But now there is trouble and there is going to be more trouble. Nothing but trouble. I guess there will always be kids on the street and while there are kids on the street there will be trouble."

Father Myers spoke to him quietly and earnestly, trying to put the fighting and the arrest of Chico into perspective. But Reno was deeply under the influence of the fatalism so common to his generation.

"The way it is now on the streets," he said, "you can't stop it. They have these what they call roving ambassadors. They go from one part of the city to another, spreading the word among the clubs, making arrangements between them, cooking up deals, starting up trouble. You just can't get out of it."

Father Myers replied with great eloquence. He told Reno he felt certain Chico could be released and that it would be proved that he had no part in the knifing. He said he was sure the arrest was made in good faith, that the police were not persecuting the Henry Street youngsters. After all, he noted, a boy had been seriously wounded. He reminded Reno of his responsibility to his friends and of his own aspirations.

Reno was obviously touched by the Father's words. He kept clasping and unclasping his hands. One of the other boys spoke up and then Reno went on.

"Sure," he said. "We know we have been wasting our lives. We've been wasting years that we ought not to waste. Years that we need for ourselves and that we can't ever get back. But these boys are our buddies, our own people, and that is stronger than any individual. You just can't give all that up. Yes. We know that it's wrong and that it does us no good. But you can't give up now after all these years. You just can't get out of the system.

"There is just going to be more trouble. Sure, I don't like it. And I tried to stop it. I tried to stop it Friday night and Saturday night and Sunday night. But it happened and that's the way it is."

The talk went on, hour after hour. There were long rambling asides in which Reno or one of the other boys recalled incidents in the long past. Father Myers talked with persistence and quiet persuasion. It was evident that he was not going to give up this battle easily—or at all. Gradually, the bitterness engendered by the collapse of the high expectations attached to the TV program and the calamity of the fighting and the arrest began to be talked away.

Finally Reno, first hesitatingly and then more strongly, agreed that the time was not one when good friends should separate, that if Father Myers was willing to go on working with the boys he was willing to go on co-operating. The moment he had gotten these words out it was evident that this was what he really wanted to do and that his other mood was one of adolescent despondency.

I looked at my watch. It was getting on toward midnight. The talk had been in progress for more than four hours. I could see that the crisis was over, that Father Myers had won one more battle to save the youngsters from the almost inevitable fate of the streets, and so I rose, shook hands all around, and went out into Henry Street. The rain had ceased and the night was clear and quite sharp. Except for the street lights Henry Street was in darkness. After I had walked to the corner I turned and looked back over my shoulder. The lights from Father Myers' study gleamed out from the gray walls of St. Augustine's and cut a bright path across Henry Street. I understood as I walked on to the subway a good deal better how apposite was the title which Father Myers had given to the book he wrote about his work, *Light in a Dark Street.*

13

cross country

Two or three years ago a rabbi in one of the poorer sections of Boston was murdered, apparently by a gang of Negro boys. The crime aroused the city. Newspapers launched investigations. There were demands for drastic action, especially after one paper published a sensational series telling how teen-age gangs were terrorizing certain neighborhoods.

As a result of this civic indignation a special youth program was started in the area where the killing occurred, a badly deteriorated neighborhood with a population of something over 100,000.

The program in Boston closely resembles that of the Youth Board in New York. Seven workers were put on the street to establish contact with teen-age gangs. What they found afforded no surprises to anyone familiar with teen-age activity in New York.

The workers reported that relations between the gangs reminded them of those of Indian tribes or Balkan states—shifting alliances, hostility and frequent recourse to the warpath in order to maintain "rep" or enhance status. The concept of "chicken" dominated adolescent psychology. Boys were frightened to go into gang fights but they were more frightened of being labeled cowards by their companions. Internal divisions of gangs followed the pattern of New York. In a typical gang, called the Outlaws, reported Walter B. Miller, one of the social experts involved in the Boston project, there were four divisions of boys—midgets, juniors, intermediates and seniors. There were two girl divisions, the Outlawettes and the Little Outlawettes.

The employment of weapons, tactics in deadly gang combat, dress (leather jackets, blue jeans), argot and individual attitudes were so similar that the Boston youngsters could have traded places with any outfit in the lower Bronx or upper Manhattan without anyone being the wiser.

The reaction of the Boston kids to the street workers was the same as is found in New York. First there were suspicion and hostility—fear of a connection with the police. Then came deepening dependence and attachment. Gangs to which no worker was assigned complained (as they often do in New York). "We want a social worker, too," they said. The worker came to represent an element of stability in an otherwise completely unstable life.

As a worker's influence grew there developed a familiar tendency—the splitting of the gang into two segments, one portion inclining toward a socialized life, toward an end of bopping, drinking and drug using, the other unable to break its habits and increasingly resentful.

The street life of Boston shows no significant differences from that of New York. Few of the Boston youngsters had spent much time outside of the neighborhood in which they were encountered; few had connections with New York; none had migrated from New York. It would seem that the pattern of conduct found in shook-up teen-agers in New York and Boston is not regional but a national phenomenon which would be encountered in other metropolitan cities.

This, in fact, is the case.

Not long after the rabbi was murdered in Boston, an

eighteen-year-old girl named Emilie Guzman was killed in South Los Angeles by a blast of shotgun fire from ambush. In the area of the killing two teen-age gangs exist. One is called the Florence gang, the other the Little Quarters gang.

One Saturday evening the Quarters gang was holding a party on its turf. Some Florence members appeared, a brawl ensued in which the Quarters boys beat up the intruders and the Quarters gang swore vengeance. Next weekend the Quarters youngsters, armed with a variety of weapons, slipped into Florence territory and hid in some shrubbery near a spot where the Florence group had a hangout.

Soon what the Quarters boys mistook for a caravan of Florence cars drove down the street. When it slowed up at the corner where the Quarters group were hidden they began to shoot. A blast from a shotgun killed a girl in the third car. The gunmen then found they had made an error. The cars were not Florence cars at all, and Emilie Guzman who was killed was a Quarters girl, a friend of one of the boys in ambush.

This was the fourth killing in the history of bopping between the Florence and Quarters gangs. During 1957 the Los Angeles sheriff's office estimates that juvenile gangs in the county were responsible for eight murders and two hundred assaults as well as an unrecorded total of rapes, car thefts and narcotics violations.

What distinguishes the Los Angeles violence from that in New York is the use of cars. Los Angeles is a city of automobiles. It is natural that youngsters bring their cars into their gang warfare. The sheriff's office estimates that there are about 160 gangs in the county, having about 5,000 members. Captain Robert L. Summers of the Crime Prevention Bureau says that another 400 groups exist which sometimes engage in antisocial activities but generally do not violate the law. There are about 1,200 adolescent car clubs, some of which are merely motorized street gangs. These are the youngsters who employ their automobiles as lethal weapons, running each other off the sides of highways and marauding highway restaurants and service facilities.

Street conflict in Los Angeles is not new. In the early 1940's it was worse than today. These were the days of the "zoot suit" riots which erupted in 1943 between teen-age gang boys and young servicemen. Emergency youth projects were put into the streets at that time. They discovered a well-developed structure of gang life. There were both boy gangs and girl gangs, usually called pachucos and pachucas. Many but not all were Mexican or Mexican-American youngsters.

The girls dressed in stereotyped fashion—slacks or short tight skirts, white shoes, white pulled-up bobby socks, heavy lipstick and high pompadours over their foreheads. The boys dressed in the zoot-suit fashion of that time. Many were addicted to marijuana and dope.

The gangs had names, sometimes taken from the street or neighborhood where they were located. Among the gangs active a few years ago were the Marianna Cherries, the Big First, Little First, White Fence, Monsters, Flats and El Hogos. Many of these names are still used by gangs in Los Angeles.

The concept of turf was well established. The gangs fought over girls, violations of territory, or to enhance "rep." Youngsters who moved out of the neighborhood often traveled long distances to be with their gang during the evenings. Youngsters were beaten and tortured to force them into the gang. Gangs indulged in much petty thievery to get money for liquor, marijuana or dope. They utilized adults to buy their wine since they were below the legal age for purchases. Leaders were called Rifas.

The same general rules apply to today's gangs. Captain Summers notes that gang members must prove their loyalty to the gang by committing a theft, rape or assault or by taking a beating, depending upon the tradition of the group. Members move through the same age classes as in New York—

—Tinies (13-15), Sharks (14-18), Cherries (15-20), and Veterans.

Girl gangs and girl affiliates are more common and more structured than in New York. In one girl gang which is now active in the East Los Angeles area, girls are initiated into the group by submitting to a beating from the other girls and by smoking marijuana.

In both Los Angeles and San Francisco girl gangs the traditions of sexual promiscuity established in wartime have persisted. One of the most difficult wartime problems in both cities was the teen-age pickup, the fourteen- or fifteen-year-old girl who spent her evenings picking up one youthful serviceman after another. These girls were not prostitutes in the ordinary sense of the word. They seldom were paid by the boys. It was, in a sense, a teen-age avocation. Naturally, the girls often became pregnant. They had no idea who might be the father of the babies since they might have intercourse with four, five or six boys in an evening. The term "club babies" was devised by social workers to describe such offspring.

Gang warfare as observed by the Los Angeles police appears to have little or no racial aspect. However, one gang which professed an anti-Semitic orientation and which said it advocated a "Nazi America" turned up early in 1958. It was blamed for a shooting in the Hollywood area. There have been few other instances of a political tinge to teen-age gang activity. A tiny anti-Semitic group in Queens was reported active in the autumn of 1957. It was said to favor an "American Hitler." An Orthodox Jewish settlement near Mount Kisco in Westchester County has been raided several times by teen-age gangs. It is doubtful that the Hollywood or Queens groups actually were made up of the usual strata of youngsters which comprise gang membership. The normal gang adolescent is completely apolitical. He neither knows the names of political figures nor has any interest in them.

The Los Angeles youngsters manifest the same senseless brutality which is characteristic of their New York cousins. "In gang assaults," Captain Summers observes, "all idea of fair play, honesty and compassion seems to be forgotten."

Cases of pure sadism are not unusual—the beating of a helpless old bum who has no money, the assault by three or four vigorous teen-agers upon a middle-aged woman who is knocked down and kicked insensible after her purse has been seized.

With wheeled transport customarily available, gang warfare and rumbles in Los Angeles often pit groups from widely separated areas. Youngsters may travel forty or fifty miles in order to fight each other. Shorter distances are commonplace. The White Fence gang not long ago participated in a rumble at Rio Hondo Park in the Norwalk area, twelve miles from its turf. Gangs from southern Los Angeles County have been found fighting up in the San Fernando Valley. Ventura and Orange counties report forays by motorized gangs from Los Angeles.

The armaments of the Los Angeles gangs have vastly improved from the primitive day of the zip gun and the car aerial. There has been an epidemic of burglaries of National Guard armories. Arsenals in Pasadena, Santa Monica and North Hollywood have been entered. Large quantities of semiautomatic large-caliber weapons have been stolen. Some have been recovered. Others are in the hands of the street boys. Machine-gun rumbles may be the next development.

As in New York the Los Angeles gangs run through developmental phases. They tend to overextend themselves, fall into fatal conflict with the authorities, decline, change their names, reorganize and begin to grow again. In some neighborhoods the gang tradition has been passed on for a good many generations of adolescents. It has been observed that when certain families whose children are active in gang fighting move to a new area the youngsters often become a nucleus for gang activity in the new neighborhood.

"When a juvenile lives within the influence of a gang and associates with the gang members," Captain Summers reports, "an attitude develops to a point where the juvenile is always ready to fight for his gang. He will engage in almost any type of activity they wish, out of fear of disapproval by other members."

Gang conduct, Los Angeles officials report, is steadily spreading into hitherto unaffected strata of the population and into new areas of the community. Regardless of whether there has been an actual increase in the amount of adolescent crime in California, there has been, as the California Citizens' Advisory Committee phrases it, "a distinct and alarming change in the nature of juvenile violence."

"This change," the committee reported, "is not merely an intensification of hostile and resistant attitudes toward authority of all types. The most shocking forms taken by juvenile violence are the acts of insensate and, at times, seemingly sadistic cruelty inflicted on other juveniles and adults, and on the very young and the very old."

The committee noted that there now is a long and detailed history of adolescent gang warfare in the United States.

"A new and terrifying aspect of individual, small group and gang violence," the committee reported, "is the nature of the weapons used by juveniles and youths; broken bottles, chains, razor blades and other crude weapons which seem to be chosen with a view to disfiguring as well as injuring the person attacked."

The pattern of Los Angeles gang activity, so similar to that in New York, differs little in other metropolitan areas of the state. San Francisco had its pachucos at the same time as Los Angeles. The few cultural and ethnic variations between northern and southern California gangs seem merely matters of detail. Federal Bureau of Investigation figures indicate that juvenile delinquency in Los Angeles is greater than in any other large U.S. city.

The underlying factor which has made California an area of proliferating adolescent gang activity is the mobile, migrant nature of the population. California is undergoing a population explosion. From 1940 to 1950 population jumped from 7 million to 10½ million. People are pouring into California from all parts of the United States. They represent a mixture of ethnic groups and cultural backgrounds. The result of this heavy population movement is identical with the New York picture—friction between the newcomers and old-timers, friction between the shifting neighborhood populations.

Taking up residence in a new area, as the California commission concluded, creates problems of insecurity which often are expressed in violence. Sometimes, this conflict may be interracial but this is ordinarily only incidental.

Nowhere outside of New York City do larger-scale movements of Negroes seem to be in progress. Los Angeles's Negro population jumped from 97,000 in 1940 to 209,000 in 1950 and will certainly top 300,000 by 1960. The influx of Mexican-Americans parallels the inflow of Puerto Ricans in New York. The figures for 1940 were about 200,000, for 1950 about 350,000, and for 1960 will probably be well over 400,000. Some 1,700 Negroes a month are estimated to be migrating to Los Angeles County now. The total minority group population of Los Angeles County is estimated at something over 1,100,000, or about 20 per cent of the population.

Comparatively speaking, the Los Angeles population movements are on a greater scale than those in New York because the Los Angeles population base is only about half that of New York City.

A high percentage of the new Los Angeles population derives from depressed rural areas of the South and Southwest. These immigrants bring into the city attitudes and customs which are radically different from those of the resident population. Here, too, lies a potent source of frictions.

Thus, it is evident that gangs in widely separated parts of the United States exhibit few differences in conduct patterns. But, since observation shows that youngsters in many foreign countries with different social systems and traditions also, under stress, band into groups and engage in antisocial activity very similar to the American pattern, these similarities at opposite ends of the continent are hardly surprising.

We live in an era of mass communications. The youngsters of New York, Boston, Chicago and San Francisco listen to the same records on the juke, watch the same programs on TV, read the same cheap comic books, follow the same comic strips, are entertained by the same movie gun fantasies. They are subject to the same propaganda and advertising to influence their selection of dress, and the same media affect their styles of dancing. Naturally, the Trigger gang of San Francisco talks the same "sound" as the Rovers of Brooklyn.

The gangs not only dress and talk alike. They put the same value on conformity. In this they resemble other youngsters of their age. The gang's conformity is antisocial. The ordinary teen-ager's is social. But each has a code which is rigorous and harsh.

At no age in life is the urge stronger to be "like" everyone else than in the years between puberty and adulthood. A sociologist who has studied adolescents as a class, Talcott Parsons, calls the complex of teen-age values and goals a "youth culture." He points out that young people, in general, attach special virtue to particularized fashions of dress, special kinds of music, their own teen-age slang, dance fads, certain sports, and to what he calls "a search for pleasure."

The shook-up generation with its unique styles, language, code of conduct, behavior and morals fits the generalized picture of adolescence fairly well.

A study carried out in Chicago by Harold Finestone of the Chicago Area Project casts oblique light upon the meaning of these special customs and mores of the shook-up youngsters.

Teen-age activity in Chicago does not vary from the type which we have observed on the East and West Coasts. Chicago has been an area of heavy population movement, particularly immigration of Negroes. There has been much shifting of residence groupings within the city and a build-up of tensions along interstitial lines as sociologist Thrasher discovered in his classic study of Chicago.

The Finestone study deals not with the general gang problem but a specialized phenomenon closely related to it— the youthful narcotics addict, the teen-ager and those a bit older. Most teen-age gangs include several boys who have used drugs and may include one or two serious addicts, but seldom more. If addiction becomes widespread in a gang it usually produces internal stresses which lead to the break-up of the group as a gang. However, there is a very close relationship between gangs and addiction. Boys often move through gangs into addiction or dope "pushing"—so much so that in enumerating what has happened to former gang members the categories of junkies and pushers seem to be very frequent. The addict is more disturbed than the typical gang boy and usually breaks with the gang as his addiction becomes more confirmed.

What happens was described to me by Chester Cingolani, a twenty-seven-year-old San Francisco artist who held a one-man show at the Little Gallery in New York in 1958. Mr. Cingolani is remarkable on several counts. He is entirely self-taught and he is on parole from San Quentin prison, from which he was released in March, 1958, after serving a seven-and-one-half-year term.

Mr. Cingolani was a street boy in San Francisco in the middle and late 1940's. His gang, he recalls, was much like those on the New York streets except that it was not so well armed. The boys used knives but seldom guns. Cingolani started to use drugs at the age of sixteen. At first it was marijuana cigarettes. He smoked them on a dare and then kept on. One day somebody came by with some heroin.

"I said, 'Sure I know what it is, I been takin' it for years,' " Cingolani recalls. He stuck out his arm.

"It was quick identity," Cingolani says. "Just stick out your arm. Jab it with a needle. But once you get on it it is terrible. You can't communicate with anyone but users. Fear and hatred fill your world. You can't walk down the street. You are afraid someone will see you. You are afraid one of your friends will betray you—to get money or dope or money for dope. Anyone will turn you in. Just to get a little."

The confirmed addict no longer can play a role in a gang nor does he want to. He has entered another and even more horrible stratum of the street world. But it is adjacent to that of the bopping gang and there is some intercommunication.

What this world is like Finestone established in his interviews with some fifty Negro heroin users from the Chicago streets. None was older than his early twenties. Many were much younger.

The first thing that Mr. Finestone found was that the use of drugs is highly concentrated by area and by race. Many more users were Negro than white. Most of them came from well-defined neighborhoods of high user-frequency.

The teen-age addict, he found, lived in a sharply contrasting fantasy to that inhabited by the bop. The user plays the role of a fugitive and a pariah of society, careless, ragged and dirty in dress, except for a few items—a nonfunctional tie clasp or a very expensive hat (the hat, again, is a symbol of status). Although he dressed like a tramp and lived like one the addict talked of his life as though he had deliberately patterned it in this fashion. While his own dress was nondescript he displayed an intimate knowledge of men's fashions. Dress rated high in his value scale.

Where the bopping youngster reacts to problems with violence or proposals of violence, the drug user eschews force. He plays it "cool." He moves by indirection. He uses his wits to evade a "chick" whom he has jilted or a policeman who wants to arrest him. He is an "operator" and he views all relationships and situations from the standpoint of schemes and angles. The user of force is a "gorilla" in his language and he has little respect for him.

Like the gang member he has a specialized vocabulary which is closely associated with that of hot jazz. It is a first cousin of the gang vocabulary. In this argot an honest man is a "square," a house or room is a "pad," food is "pecks," movies are "flicks" (a Briticism), a poolroom is a "stick hall," to understand or to look is to "dig," a record player is a "box," and money is "bread."

The bopping youngster presents an aggressive façade. He talks little and often with difficulty. The user displays charm, a rich vocabulary, imagery and soft, convincing speech. To the addict the greatest prestige figure is the pimp, to whom he looks up because he does not work. In the gang fighter's world there is no strictly comparable figure. The gang fighter has few idols. They are likely to be a dead street fighter or an adult gunman.

The drug user disdains and rejects work. The gang boy is not averse to work but has great difficulty getting and holding a job. Each user has his own "hustle" or racket—a way of making "bread" for drugs without working. It is a nonviolent method of making money, perhaps involving petty thievery or "conning" someone (usually a chick) into doing something for him or giving him something. He spends much time in pursuit of the dream of becoming a pimp.

The addict's satisfaction in life is achieved through his "kick." The kick is some act which is opposed, abhorred or forbidden by the "square." Here the fundamental rejection and antagonism of the addict to society are dramatized. The street boy acts out his hostility by fighting, attacking other boys or carrying out sadistic aggression on a chance passer-by. The addict embodies his rejection in acts forbidden by society or looked upon with aversion. The addict gets little or no satisfaction from ordinary sexual relations. A sex orgy or perversion is a kick. Drugs are a greater kick, involving a greater inversion of social norms.

His tastes in music and in dress are esoteric because here, too, a rejection of contemporary standards is involved. His shabby clothing expresses his disdain for conventional standards of dress. His ideals in music are not those of popular taste. They are the more obscure of the hot musicians (although the well-known late Charley [The Bird] Parker was held in great esteem by drug users).

It is Finestone's conclusion that in constructing a world in which ordinary mores are turned topsy-turvy the addict subconsciously acts out his hostility to society. He points out that for the Negro male a life of uncongenial labor is only too common. The hustle of the addict and his esoteric kicks defy the grim and dowdy world which is the fate of so many of his fellows.

The rationale of the drug users casts a penetrating light on the mores of other members of the shook-up generation. We have, in a sense, opposite faces of the same phenomenon, one basically extrovert, one largely introvert. Each dramatizes in slightly different fashion the same disturbance, the same revolt against life. Each emphasizes the extent to which these youngsters have turned against the conditions of their life.

It has been sometimes said that these youngsters are rebels without a cause; that their defiance, their aggression, their often insane violence lacks either a source or an objective.

I do not believe this analysis is sound. True, often the

youngster, be he street fighter or drug taker, does not understand what has caused his revolt, what it is directed against,
or, even, perhaps the fact that he is in revolt. Not many of
the youngsters are gifted with deep insight into themselves
or the society in which they find themselves.

But I think that when we contrast the conduct of the
gang boy and the conduct of the drug user we see with
shocking clarity that the source of the rebellion in each case
lies within the social situation itself. It can be no accident
that the most vigorous and vicious revolt and most spectacular
of its manifestations are found precisely in those strata of the
population where conflict abounds, where insecurity is rife,
where uncertainty is commonplace and where the ordinary
pillars of humanity, the family and the social community,
are debased or shattered.

The rebellion occurs where neither a youngster's family
nor the other social forces impinging on his life are prepared
or able to give him the support and aid which he needs in
adjusting to the complex problems of the contemporary age
and the eternal turbulence of adolescence.

The revolt is directed against the same elements which
have failed the adolescent—the components of the society he
is living in. The rebels may take an old rabbi in Boston, a
teen-age girl in Los Angeles or a middle-aged woman in St.
Louis as the object of their murderous rage. But when they
strike down the woman, the rabbi or the girl they are
really striking at the society they have been projected into
through no fault of their own.

Their objective is unconscious, anarchistic protest against
the world as they perceive it. They have not the wit nor
the means to offer any alternative. But by combining their
youthful energy, their brute vigor and their young ruthless-
ness they are writing with their knives, their rumbles and
their japping a bloody and terrible indictment of their times.

14

conclusions

WHAT are we going to do about our young people?

When we look at life today, the tensions between peoples, the constant threat of war, the preoccupation with weapons of unequaled power, the universal training of young men in the arts of death and destruction, we cannot fail to see in adolescent gang hostility a distorted reflection of the atmosphere of the world itself. The ever more deadly combat of the youngsters, the aimlessness with which they fight, the potency of their weapons, the development of new and atrocious tactics, the wider and wider spread of conflict seem, as in a distorting glass, to mirror the conduct of nations.

There is some justification for this view. The shook-up generation is a subgroup of our culture and this is a shook-up age. We live in an era which glorifies violence and we must expect young people to be influenced by their environment. If we are shocked by what happens in the street we should be frantic with anxiety over the conduct of statesmen and nations.

In the opinion of Dr. Marcel Frym, director of criminological research at the Hacker Clinic of Beverly Hills, California, there is a trend in the nation as a whole toward more and more vicious violence.

"The accent on violence," he declares, "is expressed in many ways—the use of atomic power for mass destruction in warfare, overpowerful motor vehicles, acute international tensions implying the threat of war, intense racial tensions, etc. These developments are reinforced by mass communication media which are more suggestive and impressive than ever before—television programs which can be observed at home, day and night, motion pictures, emphasizing and actually glorifying violence as indicative of masculinity, gory newspaper reports as well as comic strips and comic books which feature force and ridicule higher values."

The widespread distortion of moral values is mentioned over and over by those who concern themselves with the shook-up generation. They feel that the disorientation of adolescents is heightened by what Father Ford calls "the sex press—the newspapers which glorify sex and killing." Assistant Superintendent Noethen cites the "Monster Beast" programs on TV. Even so beautiful and dramatic a film as *The Bridge on the River Kwai*, he notes, is essentially an idealization of the knife, the adolescent's favorite weapon.

"Teen-agers just can't take this stuff," he adds. "As for the country as a whole—it is no longer a sober, responsible nation. It drinks vodka. You can't smell it. You can't taste it. It is advertised, sold and drunk solely for its narcotic effect. That is what we have come to."

These men are disturbed by what seems to be a widening gap between the moral standards which we proclaim and our actual conduct. Churches run bingo games and set up wheels of chance at their carnivals. But youngsters who shoot craps or play poker are arrested. Adults drink themselves insensible but youngsters are forbidden to buy liquor. Honesty is defined in the courts not in terms of right or wrong but of getting away with it.

"If," asks the Reverend Walter Donald Kring of New York's Unitarian Church of All Souls, "at the corner newsstand a teen-ager can buy a magazine which has stories of utter degradation in it and the human being is less than an animal, and if these magazines are interspersed with pictures of beautiful girls and handsome men dressed in a manner hardly becoming the Garden of Eden, how can he understand that he is supposed to look only and never do any of the things which are so attractively pictured before his eyes?"

Cheap tabloids, salacious magazines and brutal comic books do influence the shook-up generation. This is the only "reading" matter most of them know. Newspapers which emphasize violence, especially teen-age violence, and which scoff at the idea that they have any social responsibility stimulate street violence. This can be easily proved. Teenagers are great emulators. When the crimes of their peers are reported in gory detail some, inevitably, desire to imitate these deeds. More than once a gang has launched a rumble or created a disturbance in the schools "to make the headlines." Some New York newspapers publish daily play-by-play reports on street warfare. Some radio stations broadcast every line of teen-age violence they can lay their hands on. These reports are avidly absorbed by the street youngsters. Publicity has become part of the "rep" of the gang. Educators feel that movies like *Blackboard Jungle* and *Rebel Without a Cause* and a host of cheap imitations have played a role in establishing stereotypes of adolescent behavior. This seems likely. If generation after generation of American youngsters have sought to follow Huck Finn down the Mississippi on a raft, movies about the leather-jacket kids will induce imitation.

If it is world tension, idealization of violence and adult hypocrisy which have produced the shook-up generation the future would be dim indeed. It would indicate that we already are approaching that moment of which Dr. Schweitzer warned when the future of a society "depends not on how near its organization is to perfection but on the degree of worthiness in its individual members."

For Dr. Schweitzer is convinced that "where the collective body works more strongly on the individual than the latter does upon it, the result is deterioration because the noble element on which everything depends, the spiritual and moral worthiness of the individual is thereby necessarily constricted or hampered."

Then, he feels, "the decay of the spiritual and moral life sets in, which renders society incapable of understanding and solving the problems which it has to face. Therefore, sooner or later it is involved in catastrophe."

In the present state of our society the factors cited by Dr. Schweitzer have begun to take shape, but it does not seem that we have yet arrived at the critical point of his gloomy prediction.

It can be demonstrated without much trouble that our young people at many other periods in history have been subjected to strong influences of violence, turbulence and amorality. The American past is no stranger to war and violence. Our history has not been the quiet, orderly progression of events it sometimes seems in the books. We have been a nation which has resolved both individual and national problems by force. As far as the press is concerned there has always been a segment that catered to low and unprincipled tastes. It would be difficult to prove that today's tabloids are consistently worse than yesterday's yellow press; that the violence of today's comic strips was not matched by that of *The Yellow Kid*. Today's comic books were equaled in brutality by yesterday's "dime novels"; the rule of the gun and the fist was as dominant in yesterday's western movies as in today's TV serials; the contrast between pious word and alcoholic deed is no sharper today than in Carry Nation's time.

Our emphasis on military might and weaponry is not new.

If we have not always had universal military training perhaps this was because America was born gun in hand. It has only been with increasing urbanization (and the growing complexity of weapons) that each generation of youngsters has not been taught to use a gun before teen-age has been reached. If we are shocked by the sadism of Marine boot camps and Army training we should recall the sadism with which the (now prettified) frontiersmen and Army commands enforced "civilization" upon the Indian.

No. I think the origin of the shook-upness of our generation lies not in the international situation nor in the headlines of the tabloids. Such factors play no more than a secondary role.

The source of the disturbance is more prosaic. It lies in the home and in the community in which the youngster lives. It begins early in his life. It starts with lack of love and care and attention. There is nothing mysterious about it. In most cases it can be detected years before the child's conduct has caused more than trivial annoyance. Almost any good third-grade teacher can point out the youngsters who will be adolescent problems.

The child who is cared for does not become shook-up. He and his friends may form a gang—after all man has banded into groups for social purposes since early in evolution and animals do the same—but it will not be antisocial in nature. Even if he lives in a bad neighborhood the boy from the good family does not usually get into trouble, except by chance due to gang activities in the vicinity.

I agree with Mr. Cingolani who says from the depth of his personal experience:

"Home is the root of 95 per cent of the gang conduct and behavior problems. It is always true. If a kid doesn't get it at home he goes to the street and gets it from the boys he finds there."

When Mr. Cingolani was ten his older brother came home

from a tuberculosis sanatorium. The brother got all the family's attention.

"My father and mother didn't bring me into the picture," he remembers. "They didn't tell me my responsibility. They were just terribly worried my brother would have a relapse. This led me to the street where the tough guys hang out. I had to be the toughest. It was the only way I could get any identity. The only way I could feel big was in the group. Whatever they did, I had to top it."

No psychologist could give you a more succinct statement of cause and effect. Nor is Mr. Cingolani's proposed remedy to be lightly dismissed.

"When a kid first gets into trouble," he suggests, "I'd like to see the judge tell his mother—either the boy goes to reform school or the family accepts psychiatry—the family, not just the boy. There's got to be some force to see that they do it. This way they'd be glad to take it. It would keep their kid out of reform school."

When we shift focus away from the world and its complexities and concentrate on the family and the community we find not vast questions, the very scope of which escapes us, but bread-and-butter, well-known problems—problems we can understand and solve.

I have no doubt that violent juvenile delinquency can be reduced to modest proportions, rapidly, without staggering cost or titanic effort, simply by employing techniques which we very well know and institutions which already exist. The principal ingredients needed are common sense, civic leadership and community responsibility.

There is no place where this is more vividly apparent than in New York. Here is a city where the problem of teen-age violence has been increasing in seriousness for about fifteen years. Here is a city where excellent work with adolescents is being done, where there is an abundance of skills and agencies capable of tackling these problems. No city in the country has financial resources so vast, a reservoir of trained talents so great, a concentration of spiritual force so rich.

Why, then, do juvenile delinquency and street fighting grow?

The answer is shameful. No comprehensive, co-ordinated, vigorous effort is being made to apply on a city-wide, year-in, year-out basis known methods for improving the conduct of the young. New York is just not doing the plain, simple and often extremely inexpensive things that thousands of workers have repeatedly demonstrated will effectively reduce delinquency and halt its development at the source—the neighborhood and the family where it is born.

We have gangs not because we do not know how to prevent them but because we do not have enough interest or energy to do the things we already know will bring an end to delinquency. We do not lack knowledge. We lack the will.

In other cities the story is more or less the same. Los Angeles, despite fine pioneering, has not kept pace with the rapid expansion of needs resulting from the enormous migration into the city. Chicago has done valuable exploratory work but has yet seriously to mobilize to eliminate delinquency. It takes explosive energy and crystallization of civic demands in a megalopolis like New York to create an atmosphere in which major social problems can be solved. In the war-disoriented, prosperity-tranquilized years, too many Americans have been content to drift and "let George do it." Today, we reap the harvest.

There is no reason, for example, why low-rent housing projects in New York or any city should be foci of antisocial conduct. There is no problem stemming out of these projects which was not foreseen and which is not capable of solution, usually by the application of a fractional amount of money, a little foresight, common sense and regard for human beings.

There is no reason, for example, why any housing project need be turned into a combination of an almshouse and a ghetto. Nearly ten years ago the Rt. Rev. Msgr. John O'Grady, secretary of the National Conference of Catholic Charities, pointed out to Congress precisely what was involved:

"I have always been strongly opposed to a needs test for the admission of families to public housing units. I believe that a needs test is demoralizing. I believe that bringing together into one community a considerable number of relief families would create a very unnatural community. I believe that the community as created would bear many of the earmarks of a poorhouse. It would not have the kind of leadership that a community needs. Very many relief families are broken families. . . . There is nobody in such a family who can take any large part in community activities. . . ."

Monsignor O'Grady's warning was ignored.

To restore the social component to the housing projects presents no serious difficulty. The principal need is for the revision of some arbitrary administrative procedures. What we require are:

More flexible income requirements for tenants to prevent the syphoning off of able residents and to insure a mixture of people rather than a pure concentration of low-income, low-ability families.

Active social work to reduce conflict in housing areas, provision of flats for displaced residents in new projects, joint community organizations of new and old residents.

Active social programs to improve the housekeeping and family life habits of housing tenants, encouragement of inter-tenant organizations and an end to punitive evictions.

These changes would cost far less than the extra police, deterioration, vandalism and human loss which occurs when principles of humanity are violated. In many American cities public housing projects are strengthening and invigorating blighted areas. Failure so to use them is criminal irresponsibility—a crime far worse than most committed by adolescents since it damages so many more people.

The architectural design and concept of many low-rent housing projects has fallen as low as the social concept. Why should we build forbidding twenty-story barracks, devoid of human facilities, barren of stores and service establishments, naked of beauty? Do we think the poor do not deserve cleanliness of line, artistry of setting? Is it really true that economy and loveliness are incompatible? Nowhere in the world except in Russia or Albania have I seen public housing so ungracious, so lacking in imagination, so denuded of the amenities of life. The experience of some of the New York projects and of such cities as Newark has shown that enlightened management can transform housing projects in a mere matter of months from social cankers to media for resolving tensions, for enabling adults and adolescents alike to live in comfort and ease. Housing projects can be made bastions of social order. This requires not police. Not new rules. Not crackdowns. Not evictions. Not even much money. It requires social imagination, a sense of responsibility, a desire for a healthy community and a feeling for people which transcends vicious political bureaucracy.

The importance of the police in dealing with our adolescents cannot be overemphasized. The police play a dual role. They are the basic agency on which society relies to cope with any violation of its rules by the teen-ager. And in carrying out their duties the police directly affect the attitude of the disturbed adolescent toward society. The policeman not only must prevent the delinquent from violating society's rules but he must be certain that his conduct does not, in itself, stimulate antisocial behavior.

The problem has been well defined by the Citizens Advisory Committee of the Attorney General of California, which declared:

"Scarcely less disturbing is the openly expressed and

acted out hostility toward all authority, from that of the parent to that of the police. The police, as a matter of fact, in this situation personify society's rules and regulations, and its methods of control; the young 'cop-hater' is usually resistant to all authority and openly contemptuous of it."

Such attitudes, invariably, result in a tendency to meet resistance with force, to feel that the only way to handle young toughs is with equal toughness. Especially in a crisis a community often reacts with the same pattern of violence as does an individual in a moment of panic. Demands arise for violent police action and accusations are directed toward the courts, schools, homes, of "molly coddling" and "pampering." But head cracking, roundups, crusades to clean up conditions on the street usually leave the situation no better than before.

The reason is quite simple, as Dr. Frym points out. Violently aggressive and punishing methods of law enforcement "contribute to violent reactions on the part of the arrested toward law and authority, and facilitate the rationalization of their offenses." When a cop beats up a street boy who happens to be standing on a corner or drags him into the station house and books him for "unlawful assembly," he simply gives the boy an additional reason for taking a crack at society the next time he has a chance.

"Conflict between teen agers and police," reports the California committee, "is often the result of police treatment that appears to youth to be arbitrary. The increased use of specially trained personnel to deal with youth indicates that enlightened communities know how to deal with the problem."

It is along these lines that valuable and successful police work with adolescents is being carried on in many Western communities. This is the approach which is supported by Sheriff Joseph D. Lohman of Cook County (Chicago), who was a social worker for many years before he became a police officer. He feels that many police departments are incompetent to handle juvenile delinquency because of lack of training and understanding.

Most widely publicized police plans to "crack down" on juvenile offenders are, in his evaluation, "mere publicity gimmicks." He points out that 85 per cent of juvenile crimes are group offenses and scoffs at efforts by police to "break up the gang." The gang, in his view, represents human nature, and the way to deal with it is to direct it through personal contact. He favors gang supervision by adults, an attractive program of activities, aggressive case work on the problems of the individual gang members.

The outstanding advocate of the opposite viewpoint is New York's Police Commissioner Stephen P. Kennedy, an articulate, thoughtful man who has pondered a good deal about juvenile delinquency. He grew up in a tough Brooklyn neighborhood and has first-hand knowledge of the streets. He is as deeply disturbed as anyone about conditions in New York. But his approach startles every expert in the field and, as he is frank enough to admit, no other police or social agency of standing supports his opinion. Mr. Kennedy wants to divorce the police from preventive work with adolescents and confine it to the arrest of law violators, to simple maintenance of law and order. He believes that the police should step in only after a crime has been committed or when they have good reason to believe that one is about to be committed. He washes his hands of responsibility for what happens before the youngster appears on the street with knife or gun.

Mr. Kennedy would liquidate the Police Department's Juvenile Aid Bureau (now engaged in working with thousands of youngsters to try to keep them from moving on to a criminal pathway) or turn its functions over to the Youth Board or the Children's Court. He would also jettison the Police Athletic League, a police-affiliated social agency. He says—and in this he is undoubtedly right—that there are too many spoons in the delinquency pot. The police, he says, have no business doing "social case work." When he utters these words he manages to make them sound like a sneer. The business of the Police Department, he insists, is "police work."

Mr. Kennedy would retain the police special youth squads. These are mobile units, made up for the most part of rookie patrolmen being trained by the Detective Bureau. They are young unskilled policemen who are summoned at the rumor of a rumble. They round up youngsters on the street corners. Their work has often been criticized on grounds of pointless arrests and pointless use of the nightstick.

Mr. Kennedy is careful never to advocate a nightstick policy. He warns that it is not the duty of a policeman to punish. But he tells his officers not to hesitate to use force when the situation requires it. It is doubtful that many patrolmen are expert enough in semantics to trace the thin line of distinction. Mr. Kennedy's position is equivalent to that of a fire chief who says that it is his business to put out fires and that the job of detecting dangerous conditions which might lead to fires and of educating the public to prevent fires is "social work." Mr. Kennedy is so fine and principled a police officer that it is possible his eccentric views have their origin in his chronic budgetary headaches. He never gets enough money for nearly as many policemen as he needs and constantly must rob Peter to pay Paul.

The argument against Mr. Kennedy has been best stated by Professor MacIver.

"Where punitive methods predominate," he reports, "those subjected to them regard the police as their natural enemies. This attitude defeats all attempts to reform them. If the police are associated only with harsh methods in their approach to errant children, if they are regarded simply as punitive agents and not as guardians of an ordered society, the great majority of our future citizens may come to look upon them as a threat."

Captain Frederick Ludwig of the Juvenile Aid Bureau, which Mr. Kennedy wants to get rid of, asks:

"Why create crime? Why make young people avowed enemies of society? Dangerous people must be handled, true. But why create hostility toward the police? It would be much better for some police to simply stay inside their station houses rather than to come out and arrest everyone in sight."

In the Juvenile Aid Bureau, Captain Ludwig notes: "We don't have any of those dese-dem-and-dose guys. This isn't any youth squad, any crack-heads department. We are in business to help people to restrain themselves. Our job is to divert people from crime. Otherwise we are going to have a hell of a time to survive."

The truth is that the police of New York City and some other metropolitan centers do not fulfill their duty to the younger generation. They maintain law and order for the adults on Park Avenue. But they do not maintain law and order for the youngsters who live in Red Hook or East Harlem. Law and order does not exist there. The formation of gangs of youngsters to protect themselves from other youngsters is, in part at least, a vigilante action, a taking of the law into their own hands because the police do not protect them. This breakdown is not to be exculpated by bureaucratic excuses ("Why don't they report the offense?" "The police can't be everywhere." "We cover all serious cases"). The truth is that the police are not protecting our most priceless national asset, the next generation of Americans.

Mr. Kennedy may be an iconoclast in some ways but in others he is an archangel of vengeance. This is where the question of the crooked cop comes up.

"Maybe it's bad for the kids to beat each other up," he says, "but what do you think of the effect on a kid if he sees an officer taking money?"

So far as it is within his power Mr. Kennedy is determined not to permit a crooked policeman to remain on the New York force.

He is right in the profound effect which the spectacle of the grafting officer makes on the street boy. Such officers in tough neighborhoods usually make little effort to conceal their activities from the street boys. I have heard the youngsters talk with envy about the police. "They have it made," one boy said. "They can get away with anything behind the uniform." The average gang boy views the policeman as a kind of legalized gangster, a man whose badge makes him immune to ordinary rules. The policeman can carry a gun and use it, take bribes, beat up other people. No one can touch him. He has it made. More than one street boy would like to grow up to be a cop—that kind of cop.

Police departments must be strengthened and improved so that their ability to handle adolescent problems will improve and so that they themselves by shoddy and shallow employment of force will not make a bad problem worse. A good, well-trained police force costs no more in taxes than a corrupt, ignorant one. And a good police force can save a community untold losses—both material and human. Many metropolitan police and sheriffs' departments already have made great strides in developing a professional approach to youth problems.

Side by side and working in closest amity and collaboration with the police in metropolitan areas, most communities need an agency like the Youth Board in New York, handling spot activity with youngsters on the street, helping to channel their conduct over into socially accepted lines, preventing the emergence of antisocial tendencies and helping youngsters with problems which should be (but aren't) handled in the home. With the scale and diversity of population movements which can be expected to continue in our changing society we must expect that transient and shifting relationships within families and within communities will be the rule rather than the exception—and plan to cope with them. Even in a city without large-scale in-movement there may be enormous intra-area movements from old residential areas to new suburbs. Wherever people are moving, roots are torn, families are shaken, communities are disturbed—potentials for conflict are created. These can be minimized with a small amount of vision. Again, the cost is much smaller than what we pay when we permit the social canker to flourish.

As Ralph Whelan of the New York Youth Board points out:

"There is much to be done in addition to the street worker program. We must anticipate movements of population. We must spot places to introduce programs before delinquency develops to the crisis stage. There is little physical planning of the city in co-ordination with social services. We must expect that any neighborhood where newcomers are entering into a foothold of the old-timers is going to be a trouble area. There must be advance planning to pave the way for newcomers and to reduce expectable tensions. In many communities there is simply no leadership. They are quite limp. We must encourage individuals at the neighborhood level."

In the cities of the West where the automobile is almost a way of life many police departments have recognized the close linkage of the car and delinquency. They have adapted the street worker's gang technique. They help to form hot-rod clubs. They set aside sections of the highways as drag strips and provide supervision, instruction and protection for youngsters and their souped-up machines. They seek to interest the teen-agers in sports-car rallies, activities demanding precision and skill in driving, and away from fascination with sheer speed. The technique has been very helpful in some California communities. Eastern communities, somewhat less affected by car delinquency, would do well to move in with preventive programs rather than wait for youngsters to start running each other off the highways.

The school, of course, has the central role in the development of wholesome social attitudes in the young. The function of the police and specialized youth programs, actually, is to handle problems which could have been avoided had society intervened at an earlier stage.

There is probably not a single city school system in the United States which is not prepared and which does not already possess almost all the facilities to place into operation an active improvement program for adolescents within a matter of weeks, if not days. In most cases all that is needed is a little money and a go-ahead order. The teachers know what to do, the recreation and interest facilities are available, the remedial teachers need only to be assigned, the psychiatrists, the psychologists, the guidance officers and the health specialists are ready to start work tomorrow if a payroll slip is put through.

In the big city the school provides the natural agency for working with children. The youngsters are concentrated there. They appear there (or are supposed to) every day. Here are the largest number of specialists in young people, individuals who know the youngsters, understand their problems and know how to help them. Here is where, by and large, the best work with youngsters is already being done.

There are few programs, in the average community, which could not be financed with a percentage of the money set aside for the current construction program. Less grandiose gymnasiums, more simplicity in lunchroom facilities and a little more use of "obsolete" quarters would provide, in most cases, a pool of funds sufficient to finance most of the things which are needed to prevent adolescent delinquency.

Dr. William Jansen, New York's retiring school director, is right when he says that society must take the blame, rather than the schools, for the situation in which we find our young people. He is also right in placing the source of the difficulty in the home and in the weakening of the family unit. And there is no doubt, as he says, that families have tended to shift the burden over to the schools without making provision for the costs. However, educators, Dr. Jansen among them, must share the responsibility for the use to which they put the public funds which they obtain. City after city, including New York, puts buildings, material supplies, construction, inanimate objects first, human things —the provision of the best possible teachers and the hiring of more specialists—a very bad second.

Even so, just to take New York as an example, there already exists within the public school system every agency, every type of program, every bit of know-how required to deal with what is undoubtedly a very serious delinquency situation. The tools and techniques are there. What is needed is application on a mass basis, city-wide.

Some of the things are so simple, so cheap. As Mr. Noethen recommends, extend the school day to 5 P.M. in those areas where discipline is a problem inside the school and delinquency is rife outside it. Send the kids home tired, keep them busy. When classes are over at 3 P.M. offer two hours more of hobby, recreation or craft work. That program would cost no more than fifteen dollars a child extra for the semester.

Would it work? It *is* working already in the nine All-Day Neighborhood schools which New York now has, directed by Mrs. Adele Franklin. The schools not only handle youngsters until 5 P.M.; they serve as community centers, a core for development of the intracommunity fabric. They rebuild the community, rehabilitate the children and keep delinquency from starting. In every area where they operate the delinquency rate is far below average. These schools with their expanded guidance and psychiatric services cost about $126 per year per pupil more than an ordinary school. A single gang in a single year can cost the community, city and state far more than one such school.

Any technique which simply reduces the number of hours that a child is exposed to the street, that keeps him from going down to the corner and hanging around, waiting for something to happen, waiting for some other youngster to think up an occupation (which probably will get him into trouble) radically reduces delinquency. If a school offers voluntary hobby or recreation programs after regular class hours three-quarters of the kids, including a high percentage of street boys, will stay. It is just as simple as that. A school that occupies youngsters on a voluntary basis until 5 P.M. cuts delinquency by one-third to one-half.

Many New York schools, including an outstanding group under Assistant Superintendent Truda Weil, have positive programs for improvement of relations among races. Other schools have special programs for searching out children's special skills and artistic talents. Another group of schools has what the educators call an "enriched" schedule of remedial and guidance services—actually just the kind of aides to improving a child's reading, to locating his home problems, to spotting his psychological difficulties which could easily be put into all schools. If the existing services of the best-staffed schools were made available on the same basis to all schools, one educator estimated, delinquency in New York City would drop to the lowest rate on record. The cost? It would be made up within a few years in savings in the operation of the overcrowded city and state correctional institutions. The cost to the community of a single delinquent child runs to $3,000 a year. In New York State the cost of institutionalizing a young offender runs from $4,000 a year up. In California the minimum estimate is $3,000. These are out-of-pocket costs. They take into no consideration the fantastic wastage of human resources involved in the destruction of so many young lives.

New York City has a special system of schools—the so-called "600" schools—for youngsters who are serious behavior problems. At present a very high percentage of youngsters simply run through these schools and graduate into other institutions. The cost of placing all these schools on a basis comparable to the best of them would be a fraction of the institutional costs.

Many communities utilize their schools for afterschool play programs and weekend play centers. New York City has 374 afterschool and 72 weekend centers of this type. The peak period of delinquency is the weekend. The critical time begins Friday afternoon and comes to an end Monday morning. But this is the time when fewest facilities are available. Not only do many play centers close over the weekend but many community houses close down for Saturday and Sunday—five-day week, you see. If centers were kept open all weekend in poor centers of town where there is no place for youngsters to go, if they were to schedule expanded programs on weekends and holidays, the exposure period for potential delinquents would further be reduced. Another simple, cheap and effective technique.

There is a much closer relationship between adolescent delinquency and child labor laws than is realized or willingly admitted by many socially minded people. These laws actually constitute a form of discrimination against able-bodied boys who find it difficult to study and whose families often are in dire need of their financial support.

Dr. Martin R. Haskell, a sociologist connected with Berkshire Industrial Farm, a New York center for boys, declares that youngsters over fourteen who are compelled by outmoded legislation to go to school against their will are a major source of trouble for teachers, their classmates and society. Many of these boys have only second-, third- or fourth-grade reading ability. They cannot keep up with their classes. They can get attention only by mischief or violence.

Dr. Haskell believes the child labor laws are designed not basically to protect children but to remove boys from competition with adult labor. "For the type of boy who cannot benefit by increased education," he says, "the effect is largely destructive." Many a street boy would agree with him.

There was a time when labor needed protection from child workers. But social vision would seem to require a re-examination of these arbitrary laws as well as the related problem of apprentice systems and better co-ordinated vocational training. The time has passed when the United States can afford to squander the skills and talents of its young people, heedless of the loss and waste.

In California use is made of forestry camps for the rehabilitation of delinquent boys. Many youngsters as well as many educators strongly advocate a revival of the Civilian Conservation Corps or a similar camp system which would give boys of sixteen an alternative between the street and a healthy outdoor existence.

Already many youngsters look to the Army as a possible mechanism of escape from the perilous life of the gang. They only hope that they can survive long enough to get into the Army and that they will be lucky enough to be accepted by the Army. Actually, the Army's standards today —quite naturally—are much too high for a large portion of these adolescent delinquents. They are ruled out because of poor health, illiteracy or a police record. They are compelled to stay on the street and deteriorate further. It would be possible to set up a good-sized forestry camp program for youngsters at a very modest cost. The boys would make a substantial return to the government by engaging in useful tasks connected with conservation and natural resources. The most valuable resources which they would conserve would be themselves. It is difficult to understand why some national program of this type has not long since been instituted. If we had as much concern for human resources as we do for mineral resources we would never have abolished the CCC.

To many people the problem of adolescent misbehavior seems so complicated or so dangerous that only an expert is qualified to deal with it. This, of course, is nonsense. Not everyone can go down to the candy store and persuade a bunch of knife-carrying young men that they would be better off studying physics in a night school. But even in a big city like New York there are many individuals who lend a helping hand to youngsters in their neighborhood if they happen to live in a poor area or who go out of their way to help kids in other parts of the city. At least one specialist in delinquency, Dr. Clarence Sherwood of the Morningside Heights center, thinks it is better to have a good solid amateur worker living in a neighborhood than a well-paid professional who goes home to the suburbs when he's through work.

"There's nothing like being johnny-on-the-spot," Dr. Sherwood says. "Being right there so that when a kid is in trouble he can come and ring your bell at eleven o'clock at night and know that you will answer it." In the old neighborhoods of New York, or any city, you will find people like that. One of the best street workers Dr. Sherwood knows was the terror of the neighborhood as a kid. He understands the youngsters and knows how to talk to them better than many a professional.

Indeed, if you really want to help kids you will find a way without much trouble. And it probably will work. The thing most precious to neglected children is attention. Seeking this is what gets them into so much trouble. Half the battle is won if they find that someone has an interest in them.

Nobody told Mrs. Petra Santiago anything about the

techniques of fighting juvenile delinquency. She didn't go to any social service school. Indeed, she didn't ask anyone's advice. She just started out on her own.

Mrs. Santiago was born in Puerto Rico but she and her husband have lived in New York for more than twenty years. Down on Norfolk Street on the lower East Side you don't have to read any articles to learn about juvenile delinquency. All you have to do is look out your window.

"I see all these junkies, all these kids fighting," Mrs. Santiago says. "I decided I'd do something about it."

The fact that Mrs. Santiago has two boys of her own, one fourteen and one fifteen, has something to do with it. She was not going to have her sons grow up like the boys she saw in the streets and she didn't want the gang boys going to the dogs either. Mrs. Santiago is a great baseball fan. So is her husband. The Dodgers were her team—still are as a matter of fact. So when she decided to combat delinquency her ideas naturally turned to baseball. With the aid of her sons she recruited about twenty boys. She wrote to the baseball clubs, asking for help in getting uniforms, she visited the parents of the boys who joined the team and got them interested and she made the rounds of the stores in the neighborhood, soliciting contributions of twenty-five and fifty cents.

Mrs. Santiago's efforts came to the attention of Father Janer of the Nativity Mission, which is in the neighborhood in which she lives. Such initiative is unusual in that vicinity. Father Janer sought Mrs. Santiago out. By coincidence they both come from the same town, Humacao, in Puerto Rico. Quickly they were firm friends. The Father helped to get uniforms for the team. One day Mrs. Santiago came to the mission in tears. She needed twenty-five dollars to pay for the team's franchise in the Park Board league. She had collected every penny she could raise in the neighborhood. It only came to $22.35. Father Janer made up the difference.

Mrs. Santiago has a pushcart for her team's baseball equipment. She pushes it herself when they go over to the East River Park for games. On the side she has painted: "Help Prevent J.D." There aren't many people on Norfolk Street now who don't know about Mrs. Santiago's project. It hasn't taken all the junkies off the street. Nor has it ended all the bopping. But it very much looks as though a score or more of boys are going to grow up, staying on this side of the trouble line, through Mrs. Santiago's efforts.

She doesn't think she is doing anything unusual. "It's just my contribution to the kids," she says. "I get fun out of it."

Of this there is no doubt. Most of the people who find a way through their own initiative to help youngsters get as much out of the experience as do the kids. There is no real difficulty in gaining a place in the ranks of the struggle against delinquency. It is a rare social agency, indeed, that cannot use the services of a volunteer. If Mrs. Santiago could find a means to help the youngsters down on Norfolk Street it should not be beyond the imagination of most of us to find some way of making a contribution—outside of putting pen to check.

It is time that each of us put his shoulder to the wheel.

The United States has now been engaged in cold war for well over ten years. We have an unprecedented program of armaments. We have readjusted our whole national economy and system of international relations to meet the Soviet threat. We are constantly planning new methods of holding our own on the international scene.

Since October, 1957, we have begun to realize with great urgency that Russian technology is moving ahead of our own. We have found that Russia is, in some respects, doing a better job of training her young people and of mobilizing her human potentialities than we are. Some of us have become increasingly aware of the weight of population reserves which Russia can bring to bear in an extended contest for technological superiority—her population being about one-third larger than ours.

Despite all this few people have yet begun to correlate the wastage and deterioration of youth which we permit on the streets of the big cities, on the highways outside the suburbs and, I would suspect, in the quiet rural areas of the nation with our national defense potential. I think without running the figures through on an IBM machine that it is not difficult to foresee that the day lies not far in the distance when we are going to need every young talent we possess, whether it be one of manual dexterity or of mental agility, to bolster our technology, industry, science and defense against the greatest challenge of the age.

The most rapid possible liquidation of adolescent delinquency and institution of a program to prevent its recurrence is thus becoming a matter of national security. If we have not been interested in doing this job for moral reasons we are going to be compelled to do it for the sheer sake of survival. So the sooner we get going the better. We are coming up to the time when juvenile delinquency will be a luxury which we no longer can afford. There is no question but that we can end it. But the rehabilitation of the shook-up generation is going to require some changes in us, as well as in the adolescents.

Reno, the boy from St. Augustine's Chapel down in Henry Street, put it with simple eloquence when he said:

"If this present way of dealing with children or teen-agers or kids—however you want to call them—is not changed to something with a little more respect to the fact that they are human beings, then this problem of juvenile delinquency will stay here and will plague this city for many, many, many years to come."

If we wish our children to live in a humane world we must ourselves practice the precepts of humanity.

index

235